SPHERE

Customizable
Pop-Up Paper Spheres:

15 Paper Projects from Novice to Advanced

Seiji Tsukimoto

Vintage gold-colored Sphere. This one has a special feel.

Displaying Spheres on a mirror or mirrored surface. The bottom of the Sphere is reflected on the mirror, thus showcasing the beauty of the spherical pop-up cards.

The motifs inside light up when Spheres are placed over small LED lights.

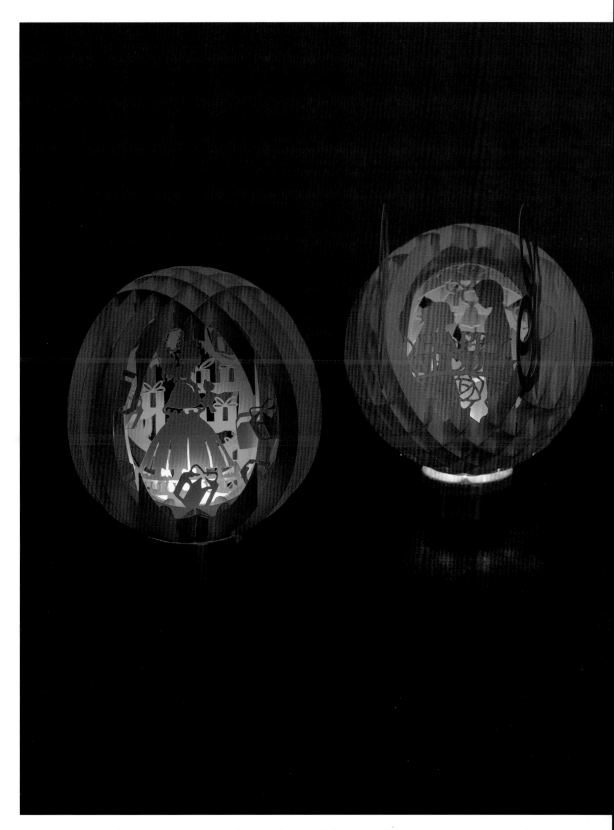

LED lights illuminate Spheres, the same as at left. In the dark, the lit Spheres really change up the atmosphere of a chosen space.

Preface

"Spherical pop-up cards" are wondrous paper forms of art that transform flat planes into beautiful spheres. When you look into these cards, you will feel as if you have entered a different world because of the depth and three-dimensional view. They are so beautiful and can be given as gifts or displayed in a variety of ways.

Taking hints from the basic structure of pop-up picture books, spherical pop-up cards are constructed by simply combining pieces of paper—without the use of any glue or adhesives. Once you get the hang of it, there are so many possibilities to create unique worlds by using just paper.

It has been five years since the first book on spherical pop-up cards was published. I was very happy to receive tons of positive feedback back then. I still hear from readers of that book, reporting completion of their spherical pop-up cards and requesting a new installment in the Sphere series. This book will be the sequel that responds to those requests! I would be happy if you discover a certain evolution— even if it is very subtle—from the previous book.

For any Sphere presented here, the ring configuration can be altered to correspond to the maker's level of proficiency—novice to expert. This book really contains a great deal of variety if we consider all of the difficulty levels together at once. Although difficulty levels vary in the designs themselves, this book allows anyone to make as many Spheres as they wish—regardless of skill level. I hope it brings you all many pleasant experiences. In addition to everything above, this book touches upon the fundamentals of spherical pop-up cards—including designing motifs and rings—for the first time. I think this can aid those who wish to create original Spheres as well as the Sphere arrangements presented in this book. I hope the designing fundamentals provided here help you create many wonderful Spheres.

This book is designed so that you can go back and enjoy the previous book again, once you have mastered the techniques presented here. In this way you will be able to experience an even-greater variety of spherical pop-up cards. I truly hope you enjoy both books.

I am now able to create works and realize ideas that I could not have imagined when I was publishing my first book. I think that's because paper art is deeper than I imagined it to be, and still full of possibilities.

I would like to extend my creative endeavors, using novel ideas, so that a great many people can continue to enjoy my spherical pop-up cards.

Seiji Tsukimoto

This Sphere was made using translucent paper, something like tracing paper. Note that it is quite difficult to reproduce if the paper is too thin.

Table of Contents

Alice's Teatime

14

Cinderella

16

Mermaid

18

Cogwheel World

20

Fairy's Christmas

22

Cherry Blossoms

26

Retro Modern

28

Happy New Year!

30

Happy Birthday

32

Happy Wedding

34

Happy New Baby

36

Merry Christmas

38

Balloons and Girl

40

Gift Box

42

Zodiac Signs

44

About Spherical Pop-Up Cards

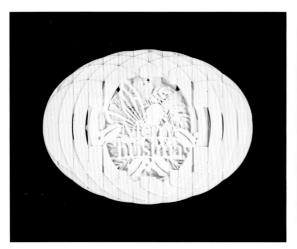 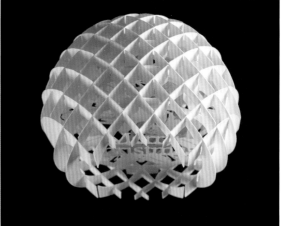

Spherical pop-up cards consist of ring-shaped parts combined to form a sphere, inside of which motifs are placed. When folded, they flatten out, but when force is applied from the side, they instantly transform into beautiful spheres. Each card can be layered with one to four motifs and can tell a different story within the depths of each layer.

Motif rings are common to all Sphere levels. That makes it easy to enjoy the Spheres interchangeably and helps you create your own original pop-up card motifs.

In this book, difficulty levels are categorized by the number of ring pieces that encase the motif rings. The "True Novice" level uses just three ring pieces, "Beginner" level uses six, "Intermediate" level uses ten, "Advanced" uses eighteen, and finally, "Expert" level uses eighteen ring pieces plus several door pieces. As you can see, the number of motif rings inside the Sphere is different and is based on the level of difficulty. The fewer the ring pieces, the simpler and easier to assemble. On the other hand, as the number of ring piece increases, the Spheres become more and more complex, which produces greater depth and aesthetic beauty. However, these Spheres are much more difficult to assemble. We recommend starting with a small number of ring pieces, just so that you fully understand the structure and method of Sphere construction, before moving on to more-advanced levels.

This book includes outlines for making the spherical pop-up cards presented here. From p. 65 on, you can detach the chosen page, cut out the ring parts, and then assemble your favorite pop-up spheres. Note that only one set of ring pieces and motif rings is presented for each difficulty level. If you wish to make multiples of each pop-up card, you will need to make photocopies of each set of ring pieces and motif pieces as shown on p. 50. Then, just use those as a pattern.

Flat Surface to Sphere

At first, you might be afraid you'll break the Spheres. But don't worry; they are reasonably tough. Don't hesitate to move the rings around, and if they come undone, just put everything back where it was.

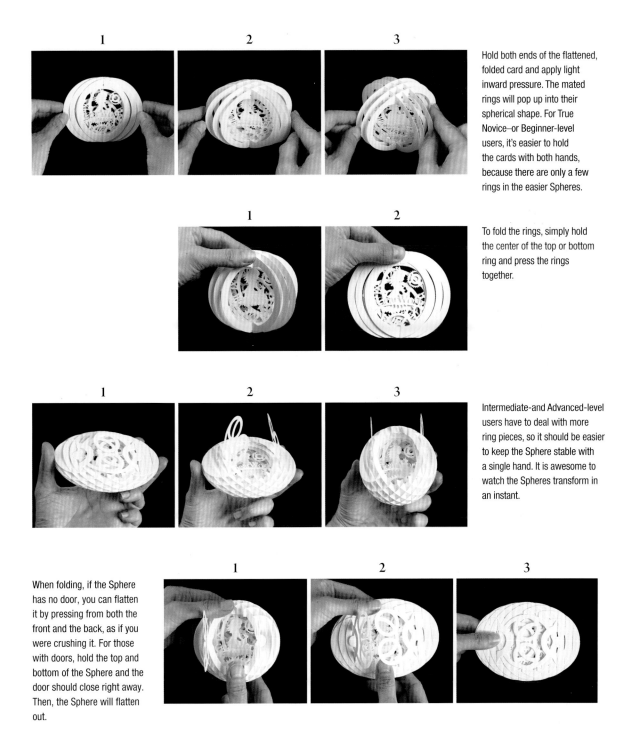

1 2 3

Hold both ends of the flattened, folded card and apply light inward pressure. The mated rings will pop up into their spherical shape. For True Novice–or Beginner-level users, it's easier to hold the cards with both hands, because there are only a few rings in the easier Spheres.

1 2

To fold the rings, simply hold the center of the top or bottom ring and press the rings together.

1 2 3

Intermediate-and Advanced-level users have to deal with more ring pieces, so it should be easier to keep the Sphere stable with a single hand. It is awesome to watch the Spheres transform in an instant.

When folding, if the Sphere has no door, you can flatten it by pressing from both the front and the back, as if you were crushing it. For those with doors, hold the top and bottom of the Sphere and the door should close right away. Then, the Sphere will flatten out.

1 2 3

About This Book

The motif rings can actually be used for any level, since the completed Spheres are all about the same size. You can enjoy changing Sphere components around as if you were playing dress-up!

True Novice

One Motif Ring + Three Ring Pieces

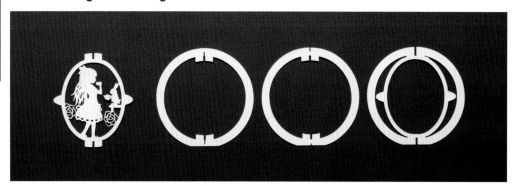

This is the simplest type of Sphere, and the motif is clearly visible. Only one motif ring is used.

Beginner

Four Motif Rings + Six Ring Pieces

From this level on, backgrounds are added to the main motif. Motif background rings are commonly used throughout the Intermediate and Advanced levels.

Intermediate

Five Motif Rings + Ten Ring Pieces

Use both the main and background motif rings. Since there are quite a few rings at this level, a stopper function has been added to ensure stable opening.

Five Motif Rings + Eighteen Ring Pieces

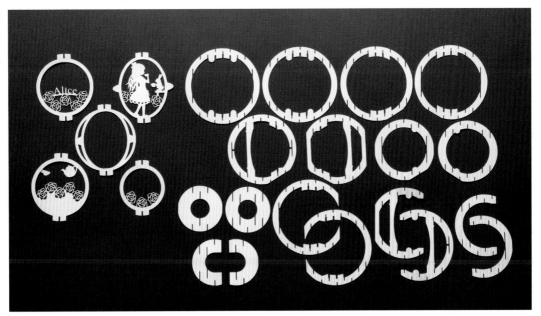

This level creates pieces of art that are almost completely spherical in shape. The rings are packed densely and can be angled slightly upward so that the motifs can be easily seen when displayed.

Five Motif Rings + Eighteen Ring Pieces, advanced Type with a Door

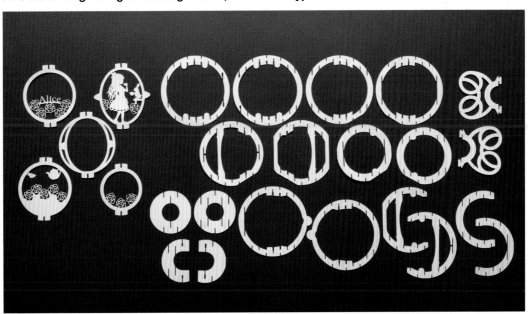

Some of the ring parts are the same as those of the advanced level, but subtle changes are made to add doors.

Alice's Teatime

Levels are compared using Alice's Adventures in Wonderland–themed motifs. In the True Novice level, the main motif is entirely visible because of less motif ring layering. By comparison, the Beginner level produces more depth because a motif ring is added in front of and behind the main motif ring. The Intermediate and Advanced levels are more beautiful and complex because the structure is more of a complete sphere. Although honestly, each level has its own beauty.

Patterns *p. 68*

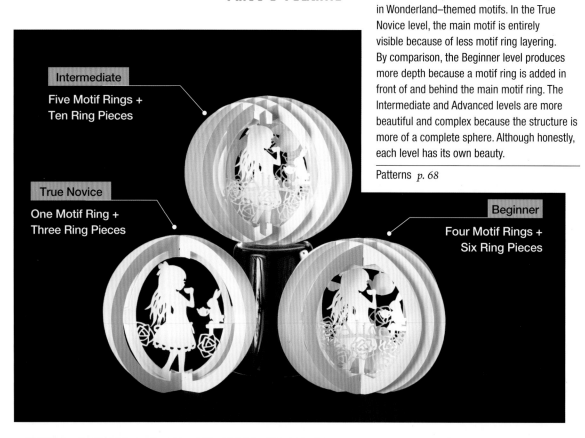

Intermediate

Five Motif Rings +
Ten Ring Pieces

True Novice

One Motif Ring +
Three Ring Pieces

Beginner

Four Motif Rings +
Six Ring Pieces

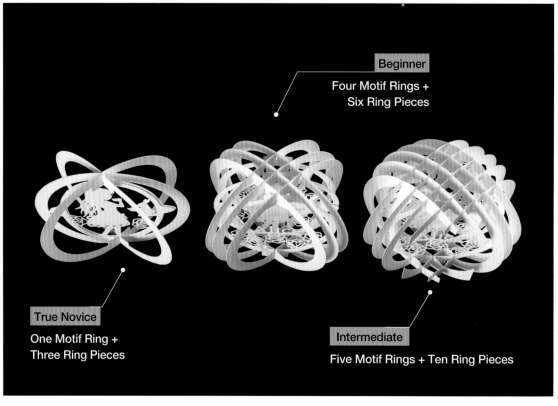

Beginner

Four Motif Rings +
Six Ring Pieces

True Novice

One Motif Ring +
Three Ring Pieces

Intermediate

Five Motif Rings + Ten Ring Pieces

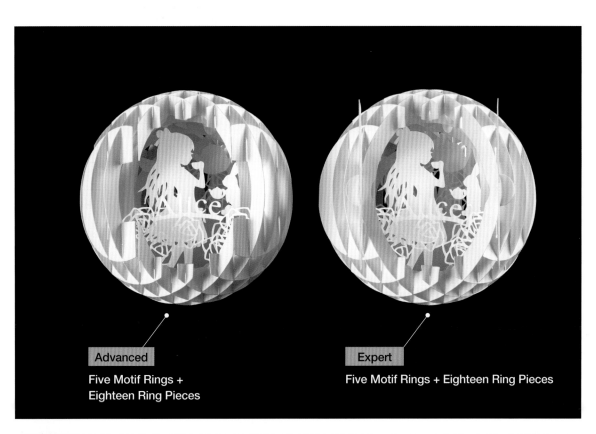

Advanced
Five Motif Rings +
Eighteen Ring Pieces

Expert
Five Motif Rings + Eighteen Ring Pieces

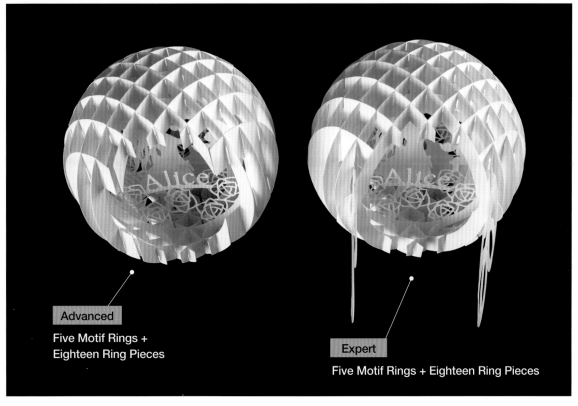

Advanced
Five Motif Rings +
Eighteen Ring Pieces

Expert
Five Motif Rings + Eighteen Ring Pieces

Evoking Cinderella's glass slippers, the Spheres are displayed on the surface of a mirror.

Cinderella

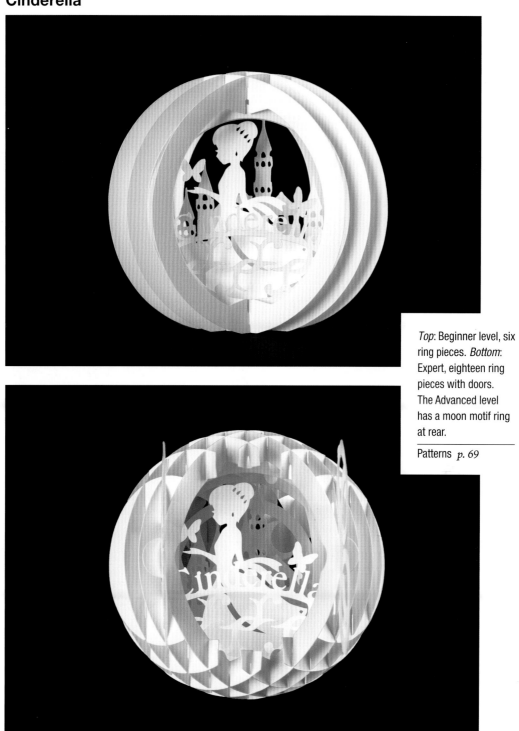

Top: Beginner level, six ring pieces. *Bottom*: Expert, eighteen ring pieces with doors. The Advanced level has a moon motif ring at rear.

Patterns *p. 69*

Delicate colored paper, in the image of the ocean, was chosen to make these Spheres. The paper is NT Rasha—a type of specialty fine paper—in both dark blue-green and pale blue-green.

Mermaid

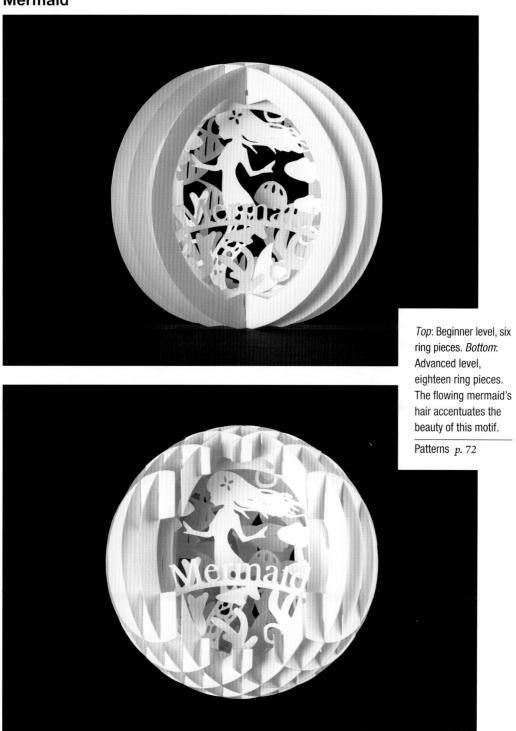

Top: Beginner level, six ring pieces. *Bottom*: Advanced level, eighteen ring pieces. The flowing mermaid's hair accentuates the beauty of this motif.

Patterns *p. 72*

Standard spherical pop-up cards use white paper, but using black paper changes the overall ambiance of the Sphere entirely. Black paper is recommended only up to the Intermediate level, since details in the Sphere's interior will be hidden.

The elaborately designed four motif rings. The cogwheels and Roman numerals combine in intricate ways.

Cogwheel World

This is a steampunk-style design that engenders a cogwheel world.
Top: Beginner level, six ring pieces. *Bottom*: Expert level, eighteen ring pieces with doors.

Patterns *p.* 73

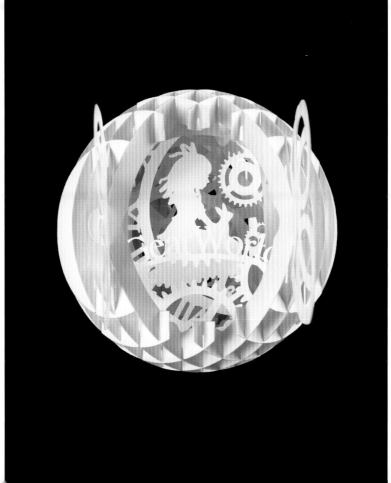

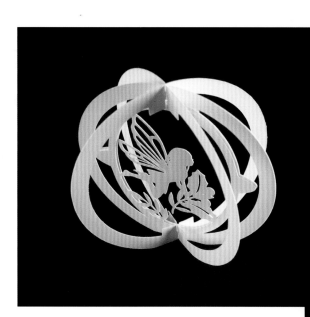

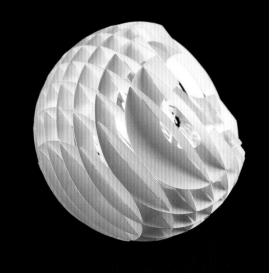

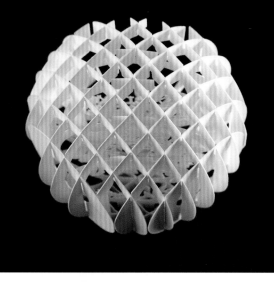

Spherical pop-up cards can be viewed from any angle.
The more rings there are, the more stable the Sphere is
when held in the hand.

Fairy's Christmas

Top: True Novice level, three ring pieces.
Bottom: Advance level, eighteen ring pieces. This cute design looks like a fairy making a Christmas wreath.

Patterns *p. 76*

Let's Make an Original Spherical Pop-Up Card

From p. 65 on, there are patterns for all of the spherical pop-up cards presented in this book. Cut out the patterns and use them to make any cards you wish. If you want to make multiples, please make photocopies of each pattern set as instructed on p. 50. If you are feeling more adventurous, however, you can design your own Spheres! This section explains how to make them from scratch, without using the patterns included this book. Please feel free to design your own ring pieces and design motifs.

How to Design Spheres

This section explains methods for designing ring pieces. Once you understand the basic concept, you can easily make spherical pop-up cards that are the desired size and width and composed of the correct number of ring pieces.

1 | Prepare paper, pencil, ruler, and compass.

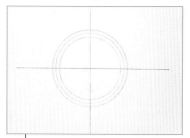

2 | Draw two lines that intersect at right angles. Draw three concentric circles—of the desired diameters—from the central intersection point, using a compass. The outermost circle determines the size of the sphere, the middle circle determines the depth of the notches, and the innermost circle determines the radius of the ring pieces.

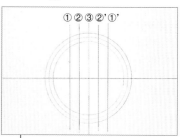

3 | Draw several lines parallel to the central vertical line. Draw the desired number of symmetrical lines, moving out at set intervals. The number of lines becomes the number of ring pieces, and the interval becomes the spacing between the ring pieces. In this example, ten ring pieces will form the spherical shape. We now have a blueprint.

4 | Begin to create the ring pieces. First, make a ring based off the left-most line ①. Use a compass to measure the distance from the central intersection point to where the vertical line crosses the innermost circle, as shown.

5 | On a separate piece of paper, draw two lines that intersect at right angles. Now, draw a circle with the point of intersection as its center, using the compass measurement from step 4 as the radius.

6 | Similarly, measure the distance from the same compass point as in step 4 to where vertical line ① crosses the middle circle. Use the compass radius you just set to draw a circle like in the previous step. Finally, do the same for the outermost circle.

7 | Similar to step 3, draw equally spaced, symmetry lines.

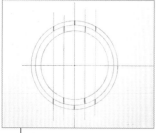

8 | Mark notches, alternating from the outside to the center and then from the inside to the center. The standard length is 0.5 mm (1/4"), but that can vary depending on thickness of the paper.

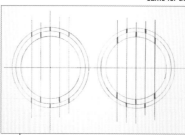

9 | Next to the completed circle, we can now draw another circle to make the paired ring pieces. Draw exactly the same circle as in steps 5 and 6, but reverse the position of the notches.

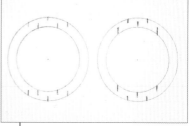

10 | Now, erase the middle circular line, the horizontal line, and the vertical lines to complete Ring-Pair ①. A pair of mating rings is now complete. Since ① and ①' are symmetrical, you can just repeat the steps above and make another pair of mating rings as Ring-Pair ①'. Then, make one pair of ②, one pair of ②', and one pair of ③ to complete the ring pieces that will make up the sphere.

Hints for Designing Original Spheres

Let's design a center motif.
Above Intermediate level, there are four pieces of motif rings, and overlaying them produces the overall composition and depth of the sphere.

Design Steps

Create a design following the steps ❶ ~ ❹.

❶ Decide on a theme
❷ Draw a rough design sketch
❸ Decide the layout of each layer
❹ Draw a final sketch

Design Composition

Use the design of Alice's Adventure (Advanced) as an example. Divide a single design into a foreground, a center, and a background to create layers. This example has four layers (rings). Each of these layers and the design has its own role.

This text is to be placed in the foreground. It is not required, but it clarifies the meaning and purpose of the work.
Message

Draw the main character—and any other characters/designs—according to the theme. In this case, the main character is Alice, of course. It is best to place the main character on the largest part of the central ring. Adding the other designs both in front of and behind the main character will produce a three-dimensional effect. It is best to use only a single silhouette for the main character.
Main

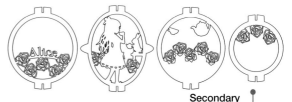

Secondary

This design serves as decoration or background and determines the three-dimensionality of the work. The roses and teacup are considered secondary in this example. The pieces that will make up the background are at the center. If you place the larger ones in the foreground and the smaller in the background, you can create a sense of depth through perspective. If overdone, this can produce a rather dreary impression, so be careful. Pay attention not to overlap the secondary elements with the important parts of the main design; rather, lay out the secondary elements in such a way that they overlap the other design layers. Pay attention: if there is no overlap at all, the work will lack depth. The best layout is one where the work looks slightly different when viewed with the left or right eye.

Let's Try to Create an Original Design

❶ Decide on a theme
The title of this work is "Cat and Flower Garden." The themes are "Cat" and "Celebration."

❷ Draw a rough sketch
Without thinking about layering, draw an image. Add any text and other elements you wish to include.

❸ Decide on the layout of each layer
Divide the sketch into three layers. First, place the text, "Congratulations" in the foreground. Next, place the main element, a cat, at center. Last, place flowers in the background. The flowers and butterflies are placed not only in the background. They can also be placed in the foreground and center.

❹ Clean up the drawings
Clean up the sketch according to the layering. Check positioning and make subtle adjustments.

Not Recommended

Here there are too many central characters. Each additional character weakens the impression of the others. If you must draw multiple main characters, make sure they appear to be a single group.

Not Recommended

Too many motifs inside a single ring will weaken the silhouette. The overall impression will be less dramatic if multiple designs are placed side by side. Keep motifs inside a single ring to a minimum.

Not Good

Even if the design is aesthetically arranged, the motif must remain in contact with the ring. The flowers at center would be detached from the ring and thus simply float around.

Regarding Placement

The contact points between the ring and design should be placed in such a way that they are attached at multiple points. If the contact points are small in relation to the size of the design, the ring will fall over after assembly and may interfere with the neighboring parts, resulting in breakage. The ring on the left is stable, having two contact points. However, the ring at center is risky because the single contact point is just a very thin "string." If the contact points are too thin, reinforcement is recommended by connecting motifs as shown in the example on the right.

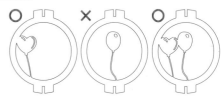

Use specially textured Japanese *washi* paper to enhance the Japonesque "feel" of this design. Pink Satogami paper, a type of special *washi*, is reminiscent of cherry blossoms.

Cherry Blossoms

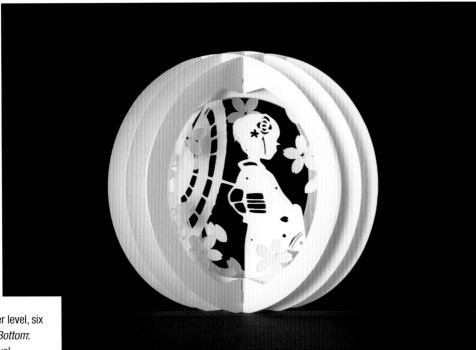

Top: Beginner level, six ring pieces. *Bottom*: Advanced level, eighteen ring pieces. The way the umbrella and kimono patterns interact alters the overall impression of the work.

Patterns *p. 77*

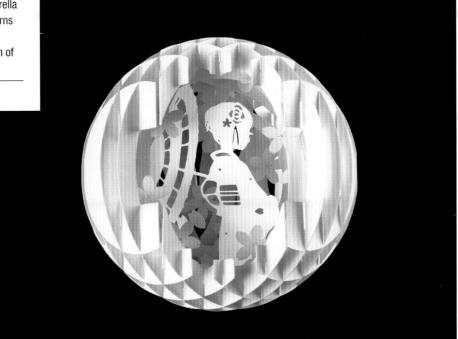

Plum and pale Blue Green Satogami are used here. The gentle Japanese colors match the design nicely.

The central designs are all different motifs, but the overall impression is cohesive.

Retro Modern

Top: Intermediate
level, ten ring pieces.
Bottom: True Novice
level, three ring pieces
and Beginner level, six
ring pieces.
The arrow-shaped
Yagasuri pattern on
the sleeves enhances
the look of *hakama*
(pleated skirt).

Patterns *p. 80*

We used pine-tree-and-bamboo colored Satogami to match with an auspicious combination of symbols—pine, bamboo, and plum trees.

These are lucky motifs, representative of the New Year. The hanging lines of rice cake flowers (balls connected with a line) create movement.

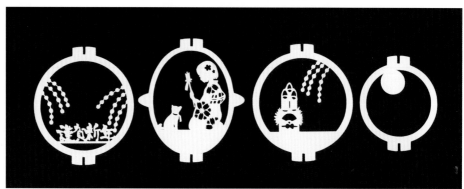

Happy New Year!

Top: Intermediate
level, ten ring pieces.
Bottom: True Novice
level, three ring pieces
and Beginner level, six
ring pieces.
Be careful not to break
or tear the rice cake
flower parts! The lines
attaching them are
very thin.

Patterns *p. 81*

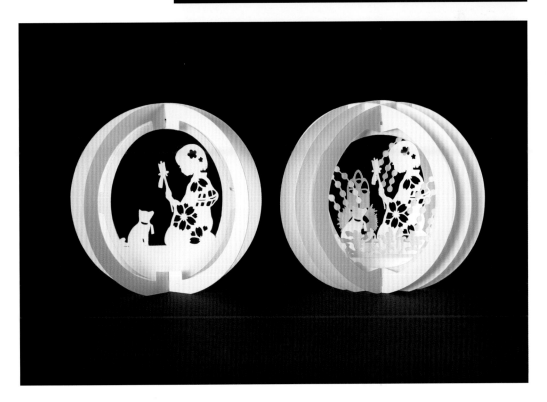

Red paper was chosen to convey an image of strawberries. This design incorporates the beauty of a cross-sectioned strawberry shortcake.

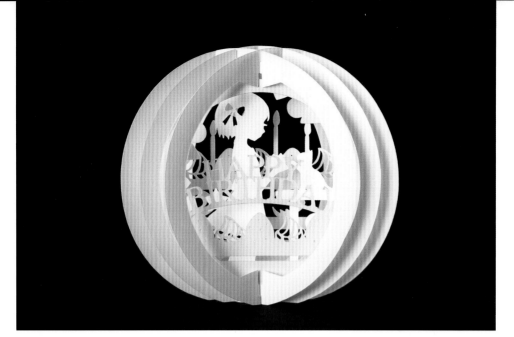

Happy Birthday

Top: Beginner level,
six ring pieces.
Bottom: Intermediate
level, ten ring pieces.
The cat is positioned
so that it can be seen
beside the text.

Patterns *p. 84*

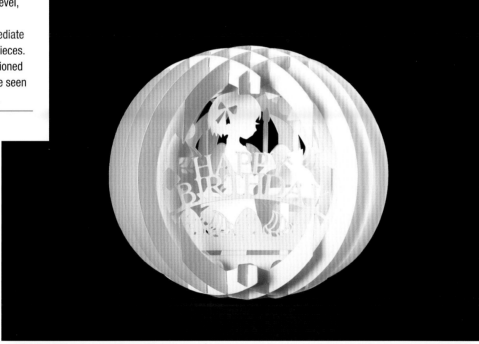

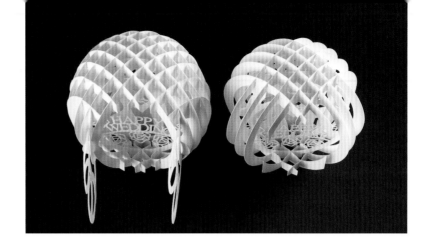

This heart-shaped door matches perfectly with the wedding motif.

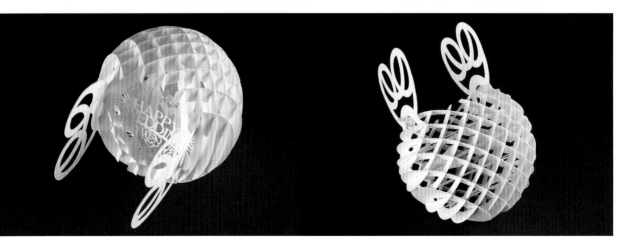

Happy Wedding

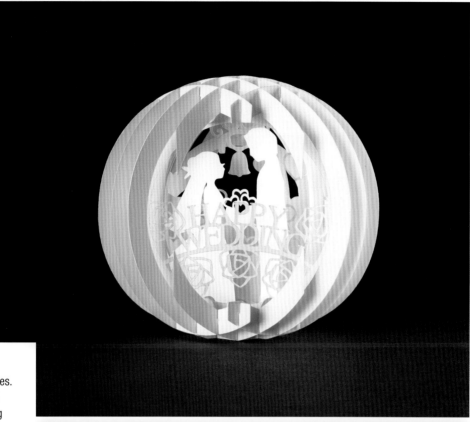

Top: Intermediate level, ten ring pieces.
Bottom: Advanced level, eighteen ring pieces with doors. When given as a gift, names can be substituted in the text.

Patterns *p. 85*

Similar to with the wedding card Sphere, you can add a baby name to create a personalized gift. The design becomes more visible when the text is lined up single file.

Happy New Baby

Top: Beginner level, six ring pieces.
Bottom: Intermediate level, ten ring pieces.
The centers of the hearts are hollowed out
to make them cute and light.

Patterns *p. 88*

Here is a cute design showing a tiny girl decorating a Christmas tree. Its cuteness will surely appeal to anyone and make them want to decorate before Christmas gets too close.

Merry Christmas

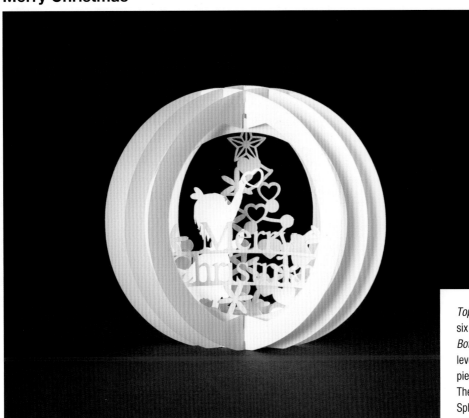

Top: Beginner level, six ring pieces. *Bottom*: Advanced level, eighteen ring pieces with doors. The Advanced-level Sphere allows you to enjoy a distinct depth and three-dimensional effect by peering through a door.

Patterns *p. 89*

The design seen here allows you to alter the text placed in foreground. This beautiful green-colored
piece is an Intermediate-level, ten-ring-piece Sphere.

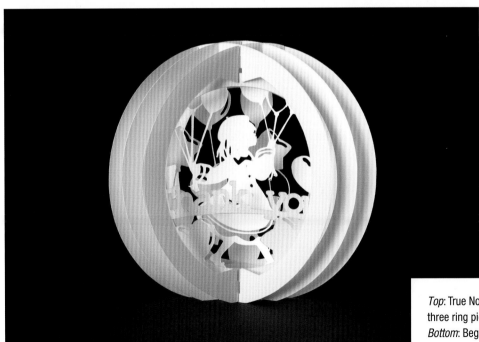

Balloons and Girl

Top: True Novice level, three ring pieces.
Bottom: Beginner level, six ring pieces.
The True Novice level has one central design. It clearly displays the silhouette of the main design.

Patterns *p. 92*

Text can be included as a message to
the recipient, but it can also be omitted.
Without the text, the design itself will
appear much more clearly.

Gift Box

Top: True Novice level, three ring pieces.
Bottom: Intermediate level, ten ring pieces.
Notice that the girl's movements are different between the top and bottom spheres. This allows you to create a continuous story.

Patterns *p. 93* (Lower Sphere's design only)

Zodiac Signs

The True Novice
three-ring-piece
version contains only
the main design.

Patterns *p. 96*

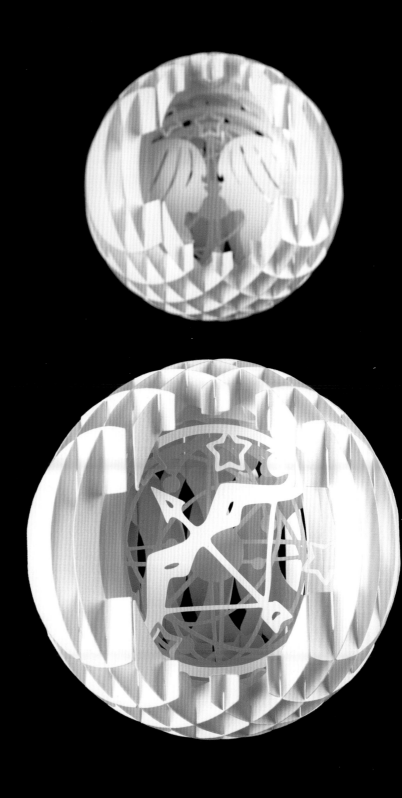

The Advance-level eighteen-ring-piece version includes star and celestial
movement designs in the front and at the back of the main design.

Aries

Taurus

Cancer

Gemini

Leo

Virgo

Libra

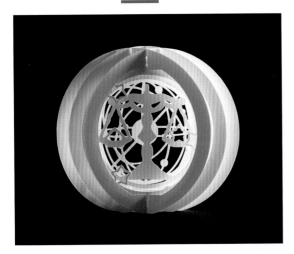

Scorpio

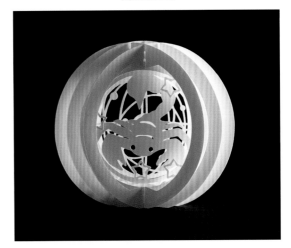

Sagittarius

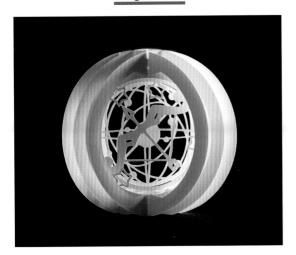

Capricorn

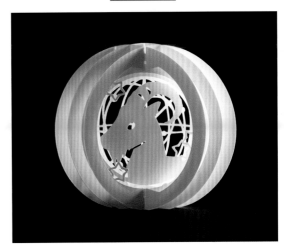

Aquarius

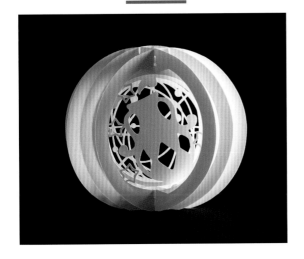

Pisces

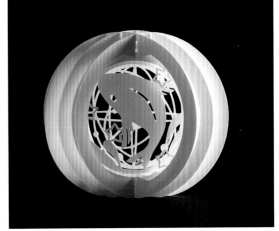

Tools

This section goes over the tools necessary for creating Spheres. Basically, all you need is a utility knife and a cutting mat, since this book includes ready-to-use patterns from p. 65 onward. However, there are other tools that will surely come in handy, and some tools that are necessary when making multiples of the desired Sphere through photocopying. Most of the tools mentioned here can be found at arts-and-crafts stores.

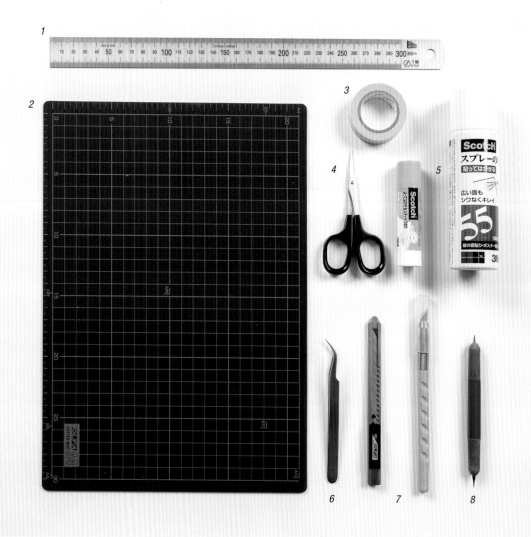

1. Ruler: For cutting straight lines
2. Cutting mat: Always cut paper on a cutting mat. This will prevent scratches, and knife blades will last a lot longer.
3. Masking tape: Used when photocopying patterns
4. Scissors: For convenience, prepare regular scissors but also prepare sharp-pointed scissors for cutting out more-detailed sections.
5. Glue: To temporarily secure photocopied patterns on paper. Employ restickable glue, so you can adjust after application. Spray types and stick types are available.
6. Tweezers: For intricate work. Tweezers are useful for removing small cutout parts.
7. Utility knife: A precision knife is preferred, but a regular utility knife will also work. Just be sure to use a sharp and pointy blade.
8. Stylus: For making very small holes that can't be cut with a utility knife

Paper

Spherical pop-up cards are amusing because of their ability to change from flat to three-dimensional in an instant. This mechanism requires a certain amount of strength and tension, so we recommend using paper that is 210 gsm or less. Note that paper thickness increases as the gsm number increases. Also, the thicker the paper, the harder it is to cut. That being said, use 210 gsm as a guide for the thickest paper you should use. To enjoy your "Spheres" from various angles, be sure to use paper where the backside and front side are not obviously different. Try out different types of paper and find the one that suits you best.

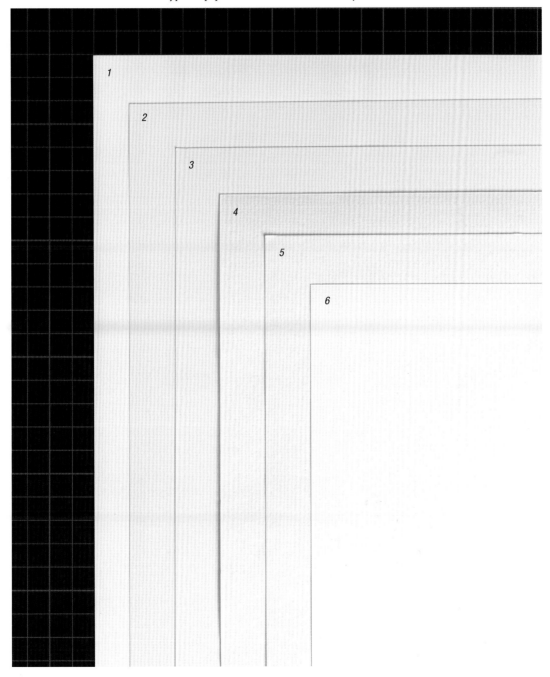

1. Kent paper, 210 gsm
2. Copier paper, 100 gsm
3. High-quality paper, 210 gsm
4. Drawing paper, 186 gsm
5. A sheet of drawing paper from a drawing paper pad, 128 gsm
6. Kent paper, 157 gsm

* Be careful when handling creased and folded sheets of drawing paper, since the creased/ folded areas are weaker than normal.

Cutting Rings

To make the spherical pop-up cards presented here, from p. 65 on, detach your chosen page and cut out the ring parts. Then assemble. If you wish to make multiples of the pop-up cards, please make photocopies of each set of patterns. This section presents tricks for cutting out the patterns, and methods for using the patterns after photocopying them. You should use a precision knife for most cutting, but feel free to use scissors to cut along outer perimeter of each ring. An art knife is definitely recommended for cutting out anything intricate.

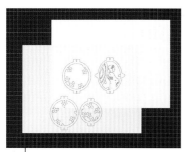

1 | Prepare card stock and photocopies of the patterns.

2 | Put a small amount of restickable glue on the backside of the photocopied patterns. Don't add too much glue, since we are doing this only to prevent the paper from becoming misaligned.

3 | Paste the photocopied patterns on the card stock. Patterns in this book are inverted, so they should be attached to the back of the card stock. If the patterns face forward, they should be pasted on the front.

4 | Secure the sheet of photocopied patterns on the card stock with masking tape.

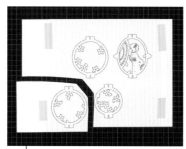

5 | Separate each ring from the others by rough cutting. This will make cutting each individual ring shape easier because the paper often needs to be moved in a circular motion to make the angles clean.

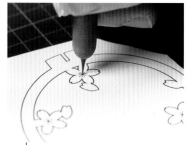

6 | Begin cutting inside the ring. For very detailed parts, such as the flower centers, just pierce holes by using a needle or stylus.

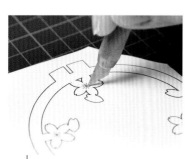

7 | Make incisions with an art knife for radiating lines.

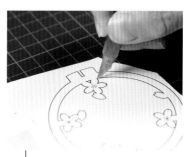

8 | Insert the blade of an art knife into one of the corners and then start cutting. Hold the paper down, but do not place your hand near where you will be cutting!

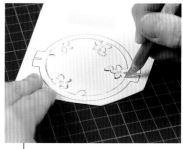

9 | Move the blade cautiously as you turn the paper, to make cutting angles easier. Some pressure must be applied to the blade because the card stock is fairly thick. However, be careful since applying excess pressure will actually make cutting more difficult.

10 | Cut intricate areas by matching cuts in the corners. Small pieces of paper can be easily removed with tweezers.

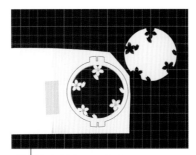

11 | The inside is now cut out.

12 | Next, cut along the circumference of the ring. Create sharp cuts by inserting the blade at the corners, especially in the notches.

13 | Once all of the lines are cut, push the ring up and out to remove it.

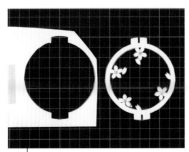

14 | Adjust any crooked lines, using scissors or an art knife.

15 | Carefully peel off the glued-on photocopied pattern from the card stock.

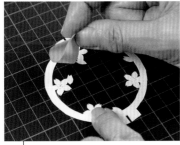

16 | If some of the glue remains, use a little masking tape or some rubber made exclusively for removing glue. Cut the other rings in the same manner.

When Using Pattern Photocopies

All of the rings and designs for each difficulty level are presented starting on p. 65. If you wish to make multiples of the pop-up cards, please make photocopies of each set of patterns. In lieu of photocopies, you could also trace the patterns on card stock to transfer them. In that case, try to make the lines as inconspicuous as possible.

Three Ring Pieces

How to Assemble True Novice-Level Spheres

This is the easiest and simplest type. This type consists of three ring pieces and one motif ring.

Since this type has an easy-to-understand basic structure, it is recommended that you begin by constructing several of this type of Sphere before moving on.

Patterns *p. 101*

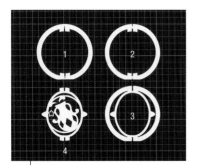

1 | There are only four rings in total. Join ring 1 and ring 2 and insert rings 3 an 4 inside the sphere.

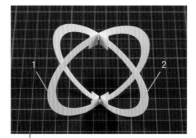

2 | Join rings 1 and 2 by aligning each ring's center notch.

3 | Next, place ring 3 where rings 1 and 2 intersect.

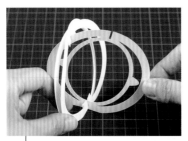

4 | Flatten the joined rings and add ring 3 by aligning the notches.

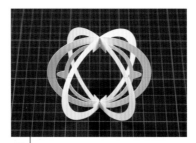

5 | Once rings 1 and 2 have been opened, it should look like the photo above.

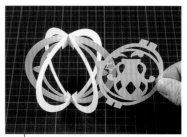

6 | In a similar manner, add ring-4 in front of ring 3.

7 | The sphere should look like this when viewed from the top.

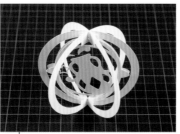

8 | Rings 3 and 4 fit together perfectly. Layering them provides stability to the whole.

9 | Last, fold the rings down and iron them. Set the iron on high and press for a few seconds to firm up the paper.

10 | Complete

Six Ring Pieces

How to Assemble Beginner-Level Spheres

The number of ring pieces is doubled here, and there are more motif rings when compared to the True Novice-level Spheres. Beginner-level Spheres consist of six ring pieces and four motif ring pieces. A ring is added behind the main motif ring as reinforcement.

Patterns *p. 104*

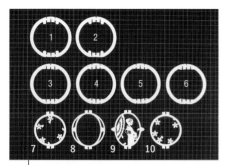

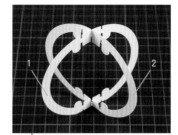

1 | There are ten rings in total. Rings 1 through 6 are joined in a diagonal grid, and rings 7 through 10 are placed inside the sphere. Rings 1 and 2 are at the center of the grid, rings 3 through 6 are the outer grid, and rings 7 through 10 are the front facing rings.

2 | Join rings 1 and 2 by aligning each ring's center notches.

3 | Place ring 3 behind ring 1. The ring is not symmetrical. Please join it so that the overall orientation is as shown in the picture.

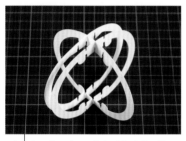

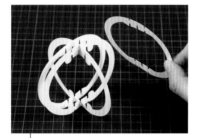

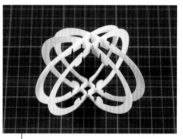

4 | Seen from the top, it should look like this.

5 | Place ring 4 behind ring 2. Ring 4 is not symmetrical. Please join it as oriented in the picture.

6 | The two ring pieces are joined behind the rings that makes up the center grid.

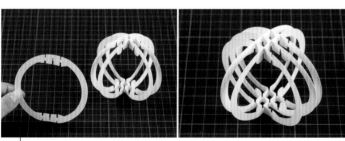

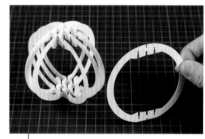

7 | Place ring 5 in front of ring 2. Since the ring 5 is not symmetrical, please join it in the orientation shown.

8 | Place ring 6 in front of ring 1. Please join it in the orientation shown.

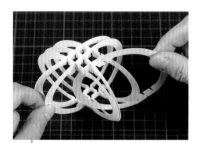

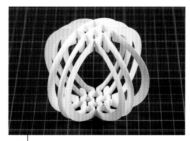

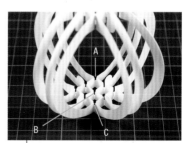

9 | First, join the center notch with the ring 2 notch and join rest of the notches with rings 4 and 5.

10 | All the ring pieces are now joined.

11 | Next, insert the motif rings inside the sphere. The joining positions are the bottom center where the rings intersect, as seen from the front. Begin with the rearmost and progress in the order of A, B, and then C.

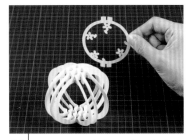

12 | Insert ring 7 into the intersecting point A from behind.

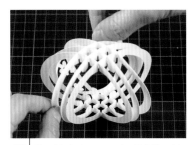

13 | First, join the bottom notch with A. Then, join the top notch by slightly bending ring 7.

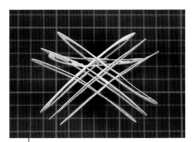

14 | Seen from the top, it should look like this. Ring 7 is inserted horizontally between the diagonal grids.

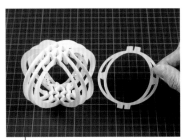

15 | Next, insert ring 8 into the intersecting point B.

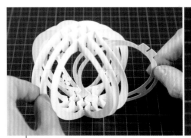

16 | Insert ring 8 from the side. Join the bottom notches first and then the top. Seen from the top, it should look like this.

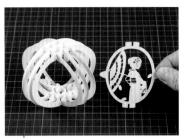

17 | Next, insert ring 9, a main motif ring, into intersecting point B. Insert ring 9 from the side, in front of ring 7.

18 | Insert ring 10 into intersecting point C, from the front side of the sphere.

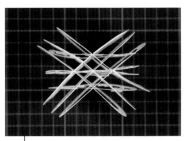

19 | All rings are now joined.

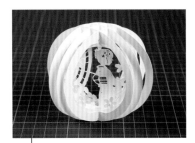

20 | The three motif ring pieces are placed inside the sphere, thus adding depth.

21 | Last, fold the rings down and iron them. Set the iron on high and press for a few seconds to firm up the paper.

22 | Complete

Ten Ring Pieces

How to Assemble Intermediate-Level Spheres

The Intermediate-level Sphere consists of ten ring pieces and five motif pieces. A ring is joined behind the main motif ring as a reinforcer.

Patterns *p. 108*

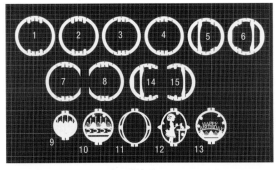

1 There are fifteen rings in total. Rings 1 through 8, 14, and 15 are joined in a diagonal grid. Rings 9 through 13 are placed inside that grid. Rings 1 and 2 are at the center of the grid. Rings 3 through 8, 14, and 15 are the outer grid, while rings 9 through 13 are the front-facing rings.

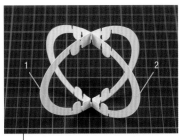

2 Join rings 1 and 2 by aligning each ring's center notches.

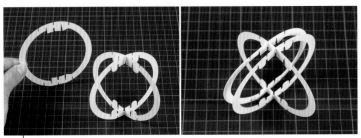

3 Place ring 3 behind ring-1. The ring is not symmetrical. Join the ring in such a way that the angled notch on ring 3 is positioned rearmost.

4 Place ring 4 behind ring 2. The ring isn't symmetrical, so join it in such a way that the angled notch on ring-4 is positioned rearmost.

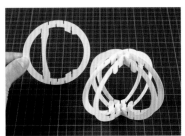

5 Place ring 5 behind ring 3. Hold ring 5 in such a manner that the vertical bar is on the left, and join them together.

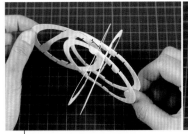

6 Insert ring 5 between rings 2 and 4. Match the notches beginning from the rearmost. When viewed from the top, it should look like this.

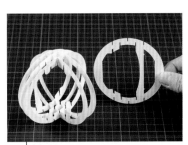

7 Join ring 6 behind ring 4. Hold ring 6 so that the vertical bar is on the right side, and join them together.

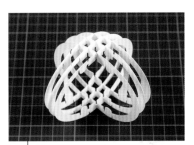

8 Now, all of the rings that form the back side of the sphere are joined.

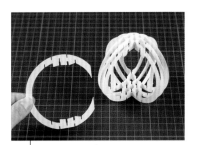

9 Next, start joining the front rings. Join ring 7 in front of ring 2. Join ring 7 so that the unclosed side of ring 7 is facing forward.

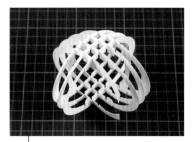

10 | Insert ring 7 between rings 1 and 3. Then join.

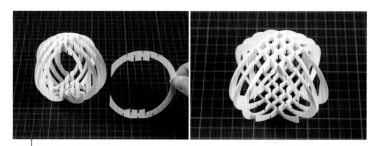

11 | Place ring 8 in front of ring 1. Join ring 8 so that the unclosed side of ring 8 is facing forward. The spherical shape is beginning to form.

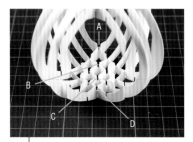

12 | Next, insert the motif rings inside the sphere. The joining positions are at the bottom center, where the rings intersect when seen from the front. Begin from the rearmost, in the order of A, B, C, and then D.

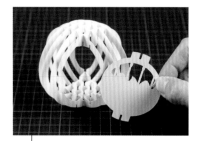

13 | Insert ring 9 into intersecting point A from front side of the sphere.

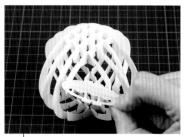

14 | First, join the bottom notch. Then, slightly bending ring 9, join the top notch.

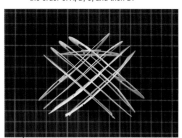

15 | It should look like this when seen from the top. One ring is inserted horizontally between the diagonal grids.

16 | Next, from front side of the sphere, insert ring 10 into intersecting point B. The two motif rings that make up the background are joined.

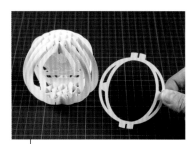

17 | Insert ring 11 into intersecting point C from front side of the sphere.

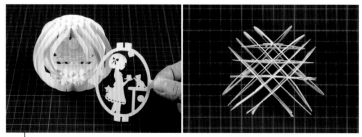

18 | Insert ring 12, one of the main motif rings, into intersecting point C. Place it in front of ring 11 at the same position.

19 | Last, insert ring 15 into intersecting point D from the front. All the motif rings are joined.

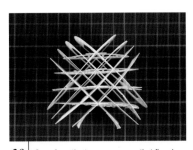

20 | Seen from the top, we can see that five rings are placed in four positions.

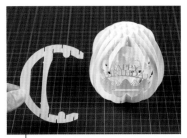

21 | Place ring 14 in front of ring 7. Join ring 14 so that the unclosed side of ring 14 is facing forward.

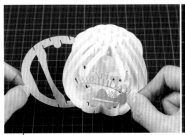
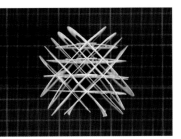

22 | Insert ring 14 between rings 4 and 6. Join the notches.

23 | Place ring 15 in front of ring 8. Join ring 15 in a way that the unclosed side of ring 15 is facing forward.

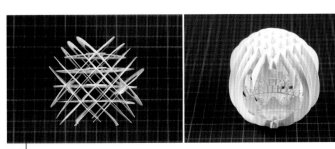

24 | All the rings are now joined together.

25 | Last, fold the rings down and iron them. Set the iron on high and press for a few seconds to firm up the paper.

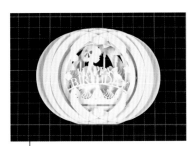

26 | Complete

Eighteen Ring Pieces

How to Assemble Advanced-Level Spheres

The Advanced-level Sphere consists of eighteen ring pieces and five motif ring pieces. A ring is joined behind the main motif ring as reinforcement.

Patterns *p. 113*

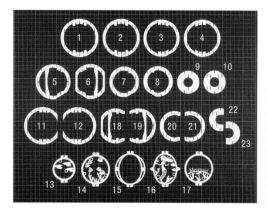

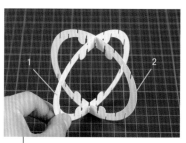

1 There are twenty-three rings in total. Rings 1 through 12 and 18 through 23 are joined in a diagonal grid, and rings 13 through 17 are placed inside the grid. Rings 1 and 2 form the center of the grid, rings 3 through 12 and 18 through 23 are the outer grid, and rings 13 through 17 are the front-facing rings.

2 Join ring 1 and ring 2 by aligning each ring's center notch.

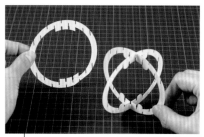

3 Place ring 3 behind ring 1. The ring isn't symmetrical. Join so that the angled notch on ring 3 is rearmost.

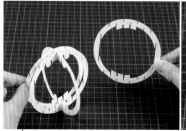

4 Place ring 4 behind ring 2. Given that the ring isn't symmetrical, it's best to join the rings so that the angled notch on ring 4 is rearmost.

5 Place ring 5 behind ring 3. Hold ring 5 so that the vertical bar is on the right, and then join.

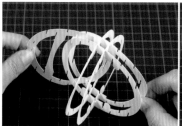
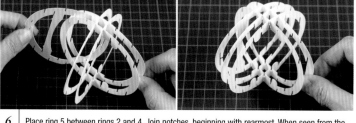

6 Place ring 5 between rings 2 and 4. Join notches, beginning with rearmost. When seen from the top, it should look like this.

7 Join ring 6 behind ring 4. Hold ring 6 so that the vertical bar is on the right, and then join.

8 Place ring 7 behind ring 5. Join so that the angled notch on ring 7 is rearmost.

58

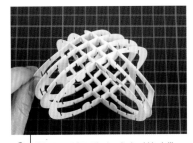

9 | When seen from the top, it should look like this. One more ring is going to be placed behind ring 6.

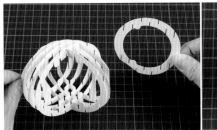
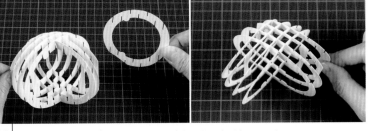

10 | Place ring 8 behind ring 6. Join so that the angled notch on ring 8 is rearmost.

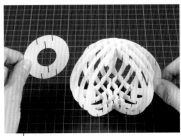
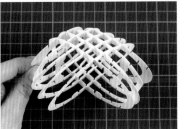

11 | Place ring 9 behind ring 7. Ring 9 is symmetrical.

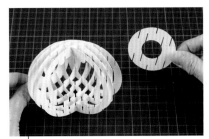

12 | Place ring 10 behind ring 8. Ring 10 is also symmetrical.

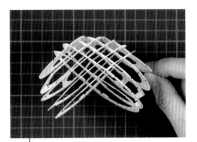

13 | Now, all of the rings that form the back side of the sphere are joined.

14 | Next, start joining the front rings. Join ring 11 in front of ring 2. Join ring 11 so that the unclosed side is foremost.

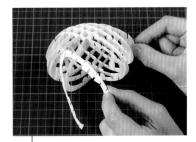

15 | Insert ring 11 between rings 1 and 3. Join the notches.

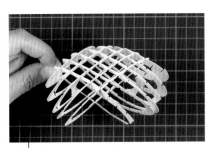

16 | When seen from the top, it should look like this.

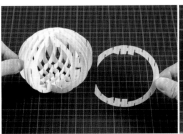

17 | Place ring 12 in front of ring 1. Join ring 12 so that the unclosed side is foremost. The spherical shape is beginning to form.

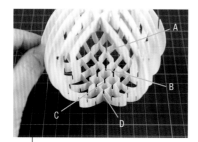

18 | Next, insert motif rings into sphere. Joining positions are at the bottom center, where the rings intersect when seen from the front. Begin with rearmost and move in the order of A, B, C, and then D.

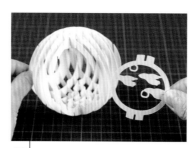

19 | Insert ring 13 into intersection point A from the front side of the sphere.

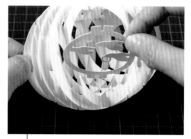

20 | First, join the bottom notch. Then join the top notch as you slightly bend ring 13.

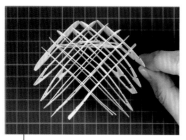

21 | When seen from the top, it should look like this. The ring is inserted horizontally between the diagonal grids.

22 | Next, insert ring 14 into intersection point B from front side of the sphere. Now, the two motif rings that will serve as a background have been inserted.

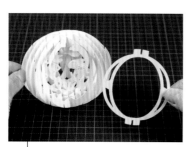

23 | Insert ring 15 into intersection point C from the front.

24 | Insert ring 16, a main motif ring, into intersection point C. Place it in front of ring 15, using the same position.

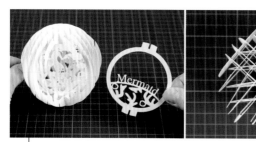

25 | Last, insert ring 17 into intersection point D from front side of the sphere. Now, all the motif rings are joined. When seen from the top, the five rings are placed in four positions as seen.

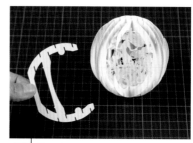

26 | Place ring 18 in front of ring 11. Insert it so that the unclosed side is facing the front.

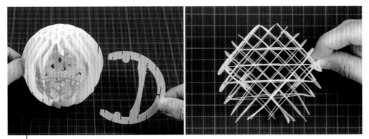

27 Place ring 19 in front of ring 12. Insert it so that the unclosed side is facing the front.

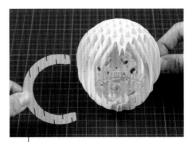

28 Place ring 20 in front of ring 18. Insert it so that the unclosed side is facing the front.

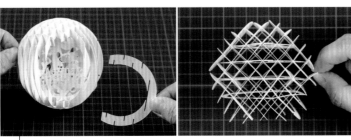

29 Place ring 21 in front of ring 19. Insert it so that the unclosed side is facing the front.

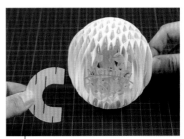

30 Place ring 22 in front of ring 20. Insert it so that the unclosed side is facing the front.

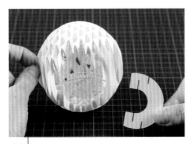
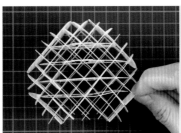

31 Place ring 23 in front of ring 21. Insert it so that the unclosed side is facing the front.

32 All the rings are now joined.

33 Last, fold the rings down and iron. Set the iron on high and press for a few seconds to firm up the paper.

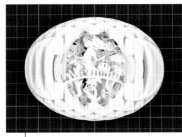

34 Complete

Eighteen Ring Pieces Plus Door

How to Assemble Expert Level Spheres

The components of the Expert-level Sphere are almost same as the Advance-level Sphere, except that it has actual door pieces. The Expert-level Sphere consists of eighteen ring pieces, two door pieces, and five motif pieces. A ring is placed behind the main motif ring as reinforcement.

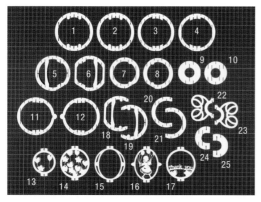

Patterns *p. 121*

1 | There are twenty-five rings in total. Rings 1 through 12, 18 through 21, 24, and 25 are joined in a diagonal grid. Rings 13 through 17 are placed inside that grid. The door pieces (rings 22 and 23) are attached to rings 1 and 2. Ring 1 and ring 2 are the center of the grid. Rings 3 through 12, 18 through 21, 24, and 25 are the outer grid. Rings 22 and 23 are the door pieces. Rings 13 through 17 are the front-facing pieces.

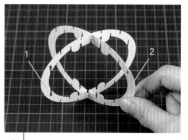

2 | Join rings 1 and 2 by aligning the center notches.

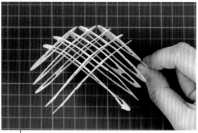

3 | The same rings as those used for an Advance-level Sphere are used to form backside here, so just refer to steps 3 through 12—on p. 58—for assembly instructions. After completion, the backside should be assembled.

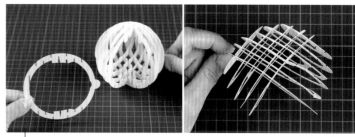

4 | Next, start joining the front rings. Place ring 11 in front of ring 2. Join them so that the angled notch on ring 11 is foremost.

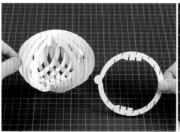

5 | Place ring 12 in front of ring 1. Join them so that the angled notch on ring 12 is foremost.

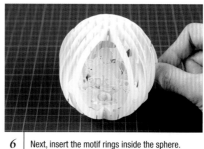

6 | Next, insert the motif rings inside the sphere. Insert each ring where the others cross. Begin at the back, moving from A through D. Since these steps are same as the Advanced level, refer to steps 18 through 25 on p. 60 and assemble in the same way.

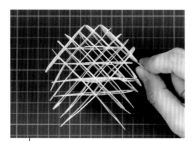

7 | Seen from the top, the five rings are placed in four positions.

8 | Place ring 18 in front of ring 11 and ring 19 in front of ring 12. Join them so that the open part of the ring is facing forward.

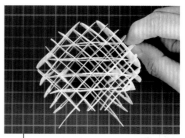

9 | Place ring 20 in front of ring 18 and ring 21 in front of ring 19. Join them so that the open part of the ring is facing forward.

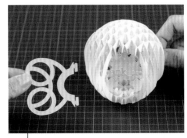

10 | Add ring 22 as one of the door pieces.

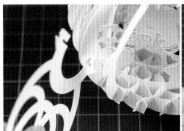

11 | Hang the hooks of ring 22 on the notches of ring 1. Fasten both the top and bottom hooks.

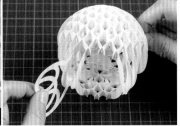

12 | On the other side of the sphere, hang ring 23 hooks on the notches of ring 2. The door is now attached.

13 | Place ring 24 in front of ring 20. Join so that the open part of the ring is facing forward.

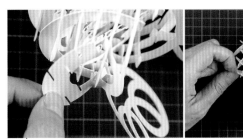

14 | Join the outermost notch of ring 24 (*see photo*) and the notches on ring 1 where the door piece is attached. This will help firmly secure the door piece.

15 | Do the same for the opposite side. Join the outermost notch on ring 25 (*see photo*) with the notches on ring 2 where the door piece is attached.

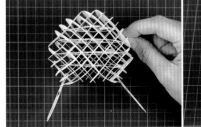

16 | All the rings are now joined.

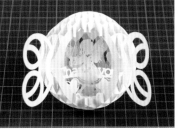

17 | Fold the rings and iron everything flat to complete.

Paper artist **Seiji Tsukimoto** focuses on coming up with new ideas and enjoys translating themes from children's classic stories, fairy tales, and folklore, drawing from his native Japanese and from Western cultures. He continues to search for and create new types of pop-up designs. He lives in Chiba, Japan.

Other Schiffer Books on Related Subjects:

Papercutting: Geometric Designs Inspired by Nature, Patricia Moffett, ISBN 978-0-7643-5808-1

Folding Polyhedra: The Art & Geometry of Paper Folding, Alexander Heinz, ISBN 978-0-7643-6157-9

Paper Joy for Every Room: 15 Fun Projects to Add Decorating Charm to Your Home, Laure Farion, ISBN 978-0-7643-6055-8

ISBN: 978-0-7643-6617-8

Printed in China

Published by Schiffer Publishing, Ltd.
4880 Lower Valley Road
Atglen, PA 19310
Phone: (610) 593-1777; Fax: (610) 593-2002
Email: Info@schifferbooks.com
Web: www.schifferbooks.com

For our complete selection of fine books on this and related subjects, please visit our website at www.schifferbooks.com. You may also write for a free catalog.

Schiffer Publishing's titles are available at special discounts for bulk purchases for sales promotions or premiums. Special editions, including personalized covers, corporate imprints, and excerpts, can be created in large quantities for special needs. For more information, contact the publisher.

We are always looking for people to write books on new and related subjects. If you have an idea for a book, please contact us at proposals@schifferbooks.com.

Japanese edition © 2021 Seiji Tsukimoto
Japanese edition © 2021 GRAPHIC-SHA PUBLISHING CO., LTD

First designed and published in Japan in 2021 by Graphic-sha Publishing Co., Ltd.
English edition published in the United States of America in 2022 by Schiffer Publishing, Ltd.

Original edition creative staff
Photos: Kazumasa Yamamoto
Art direction & layout: Satomi Nakata
Tracing: Kyodo Kogeisha
Editing: Ayako Enaka(Graphic-sha Publishing)

English edition creative staff
English translation: Kevin Wilson
English edition layout: Shinichi Ishioka
Foreign edition Production and management: Takako Motoki (Graphic-sha Publishing)

Patterns

Patterns for all "Spheres" presented in this book are provided from this page onward. Cut out the patterns and use them to make your chosen Sphere. Only one set of the ring pieces and motif rings is presented for each difficulty level. If you wish to make multiples of the pop-up cards, please photocopy each set of patterns. The side where the patterns are printed is going to be "the backside." That being said, the patterns are printed as inverted images. Be very careful when determining the orientation of letters and parts that aren't symmetrical. Please assemble the pieces by looking at the white "front side," which doesn't have any printing. Assembly instructions are given starting on p. 52.

P. 25

Original Design Rings
This is the central motif ring when making original design Spheres. You can make any design you like on the inside of the ring.

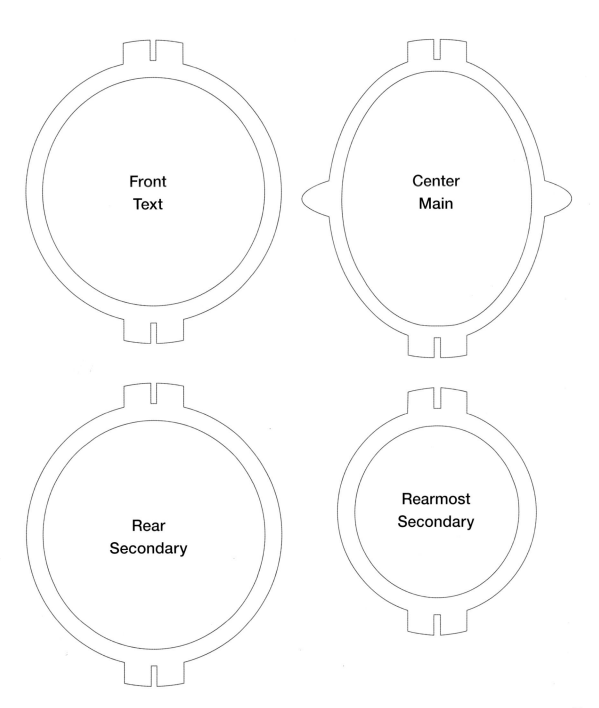

Cut Here

P. 14

Alice's Teatime Motif Rings

These motif rings are used for True Novice–through Advanced-level Spheres. See p. 52 and onward for instructions.

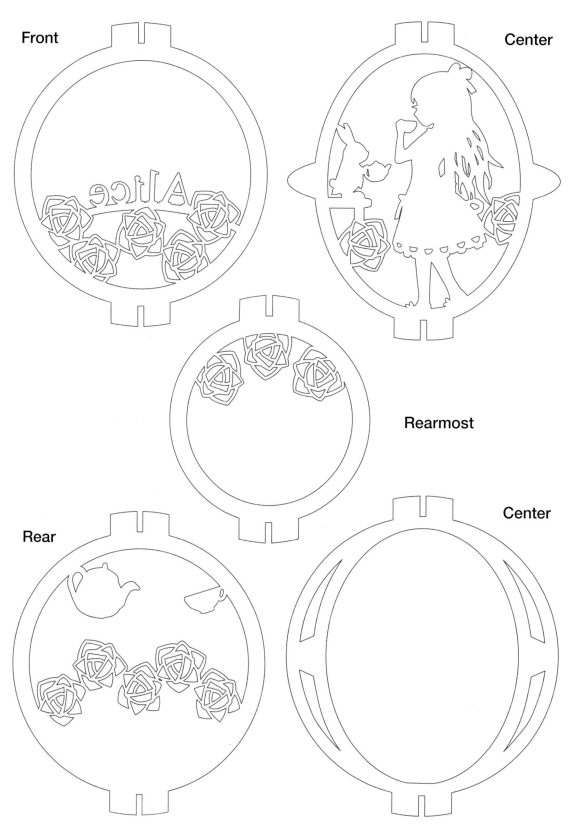

Front

Center

Rearmost

Rear

Center

Cinderella Motif Rings

These motif rings are used for True Novice–through Advanced-level Spheres. See p. 52 and onward for instructions.

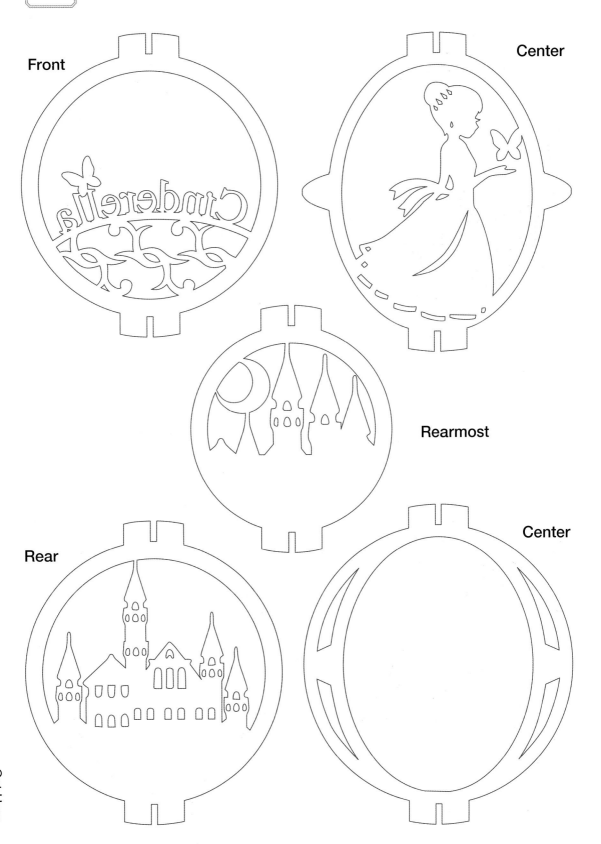

Front

Center

Rearmost

Rear

Center

Cut Here

Cut Here

Mermaid Motif Design

These motif rings are used for True Novice–through Advanced-level Spheres. See p. 52 and onward for instructions.

Front

Center

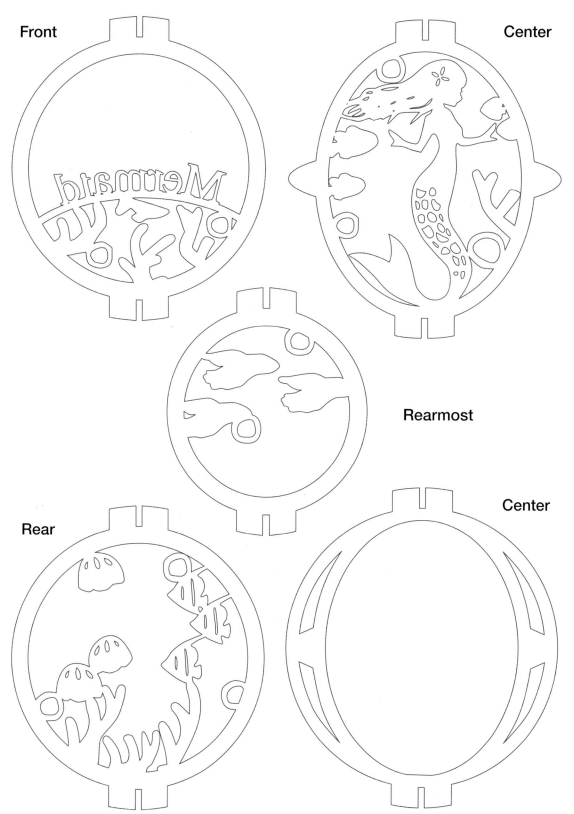

Rearmost

Rear

Center

Cut Here

Cogwheel World Motif Rings

These motif rings are used for True Novice–through Advanced-level Spheres. See p. 52 and onward for instructions.

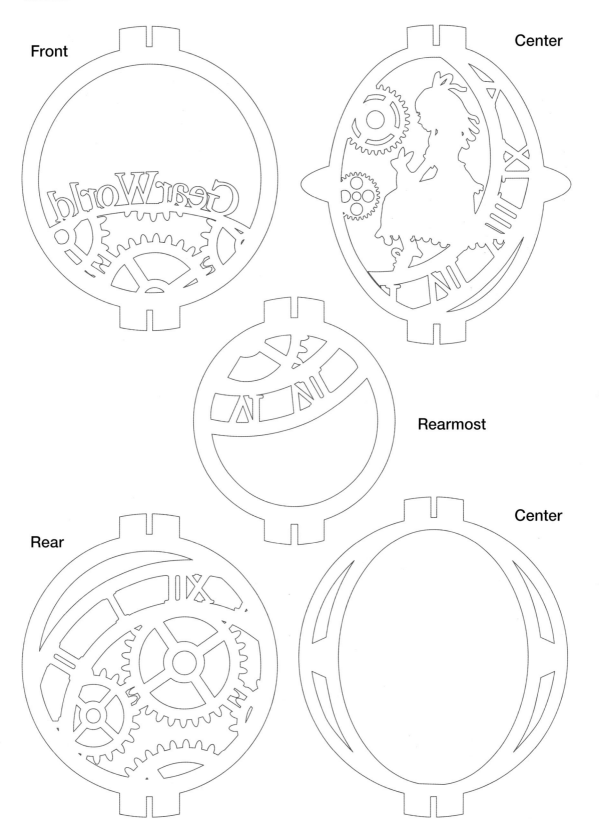

Front

Center

Rearmost

Rear

Center

Cut Here

Cut Here

Fairy's Christmas Motif Rings

These motif rings are used for True Novice–through Advanced-level Spheres. See p. 52 and onward for instructions.

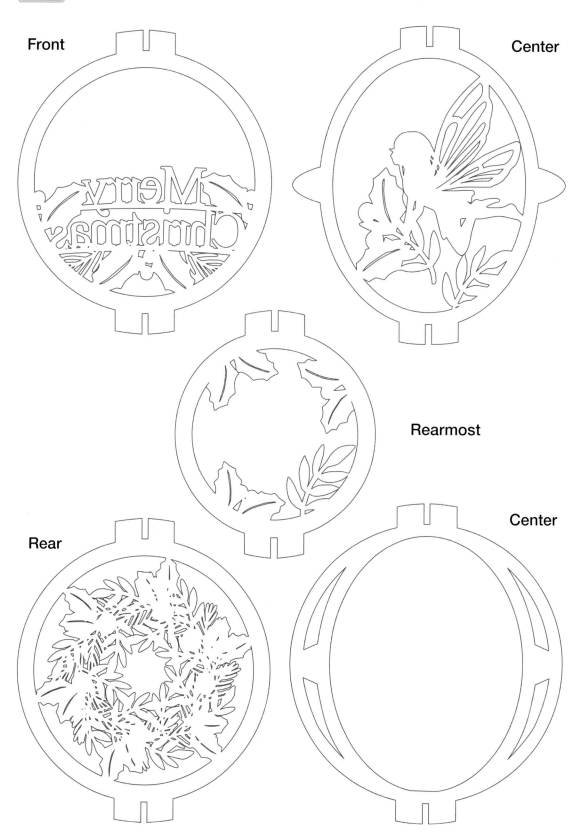

Front

Center

Rearmost

Rear

Center

Cut Here

Cherry Blossoms Motif Rings

These motif rings are used for True Novice–through Advanced-level Spheres. See p. 52 and onward for instructions.

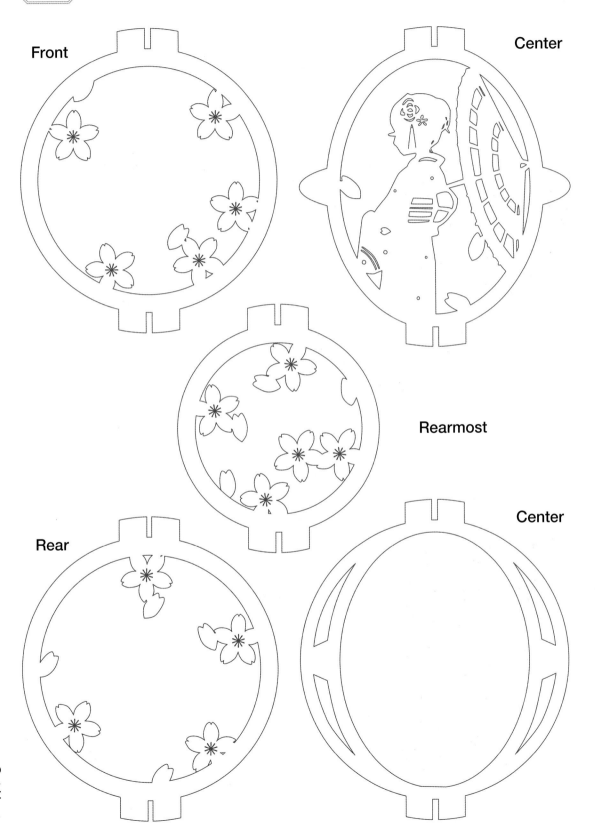

Front

Center

Rearmost

Rear

Center

Cut Here

P. 28

Retro Modern Motif Rings

These motif rings are used for True Novice–through Advanced-level Spheres. See p. 52 and onward for instructions.

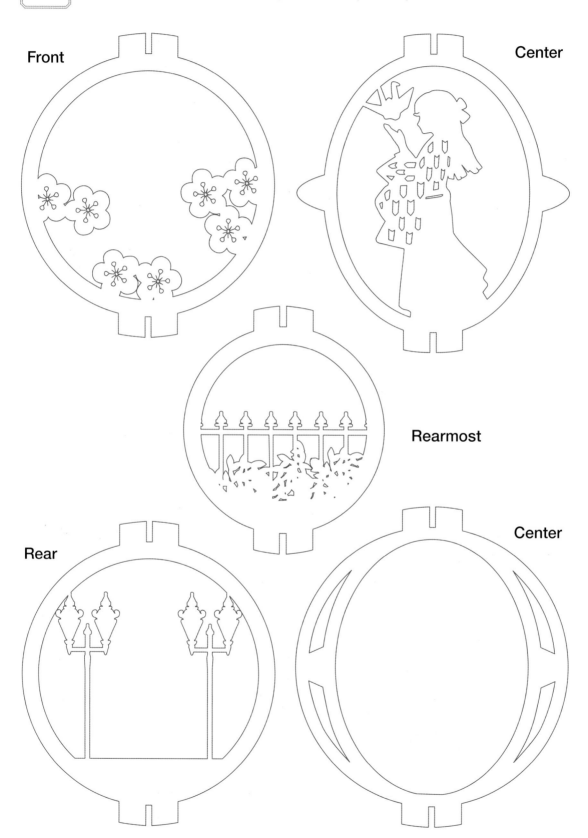

Front

Center

Rearmost

Rear

Center

Cut Here

P. 30

Happy New Year! Motif Rings

These motif rings are used for True Novice–through Advanced-level Spheres. See p. 52 and onward for instructions.

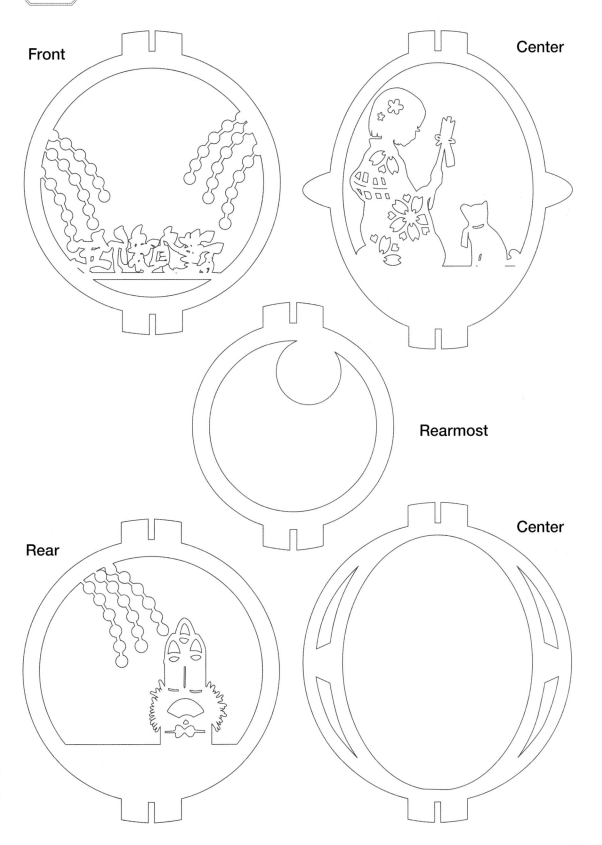

Front

Center

Rearmost

Rear

Center

Cut Here

Happy Birthday Motif Rings

These motif rings are used for True Novice–through Advanced-level Spheres. See p. 52 and onward for instructions.

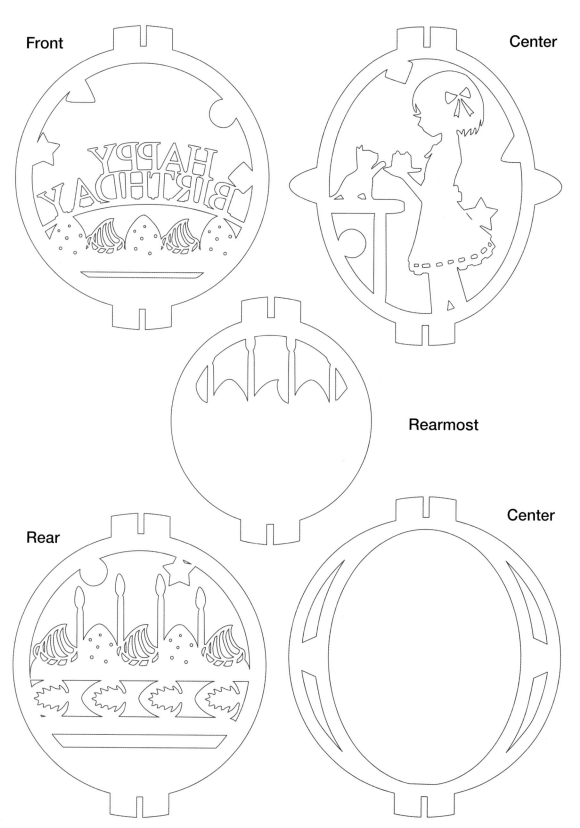

Front

Center

Rearmost

Rear

Center

Cut Here

P. 34

Happy Wedding Motif Rings

These motif rings are used for True Novice–through Advanced-level Spheres. See p. 52 and onward for instructions.

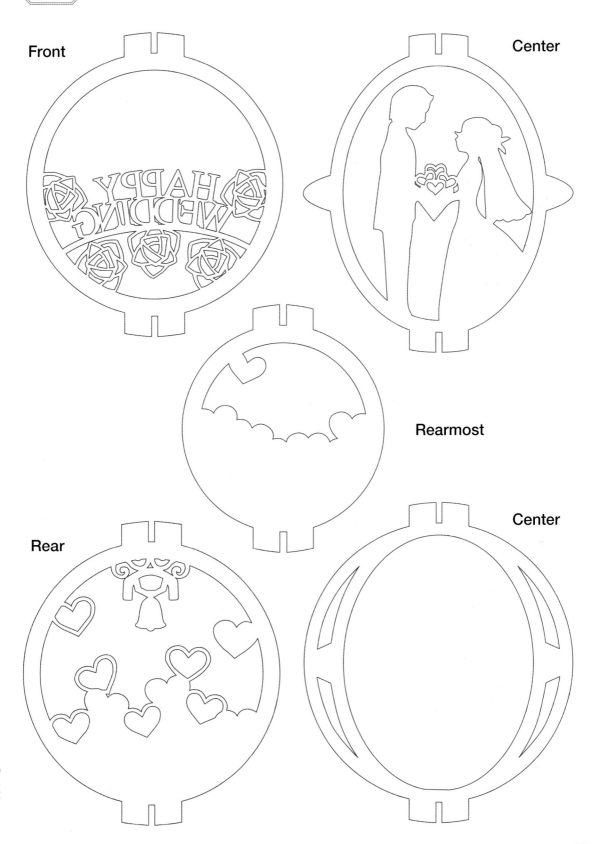

Front

Center

Rearmost

Rear

Center

Cut Here

P. 36

Happy New Baby Motif Rings

The motif rings commonly used for True Novice–through Advanced-level Spheres. See p. 52 and onward for instructions.

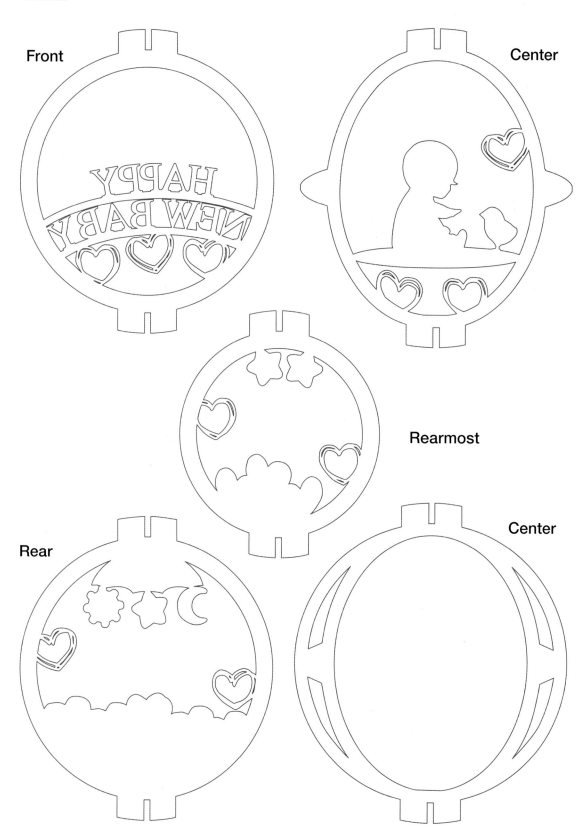

Front

Center

Rearmost

Rear

Center

Cut Here

P. 38

Merry Christmas Motif Rings

The motif rings commonly used for True Novice–through Advanced-level Spheres. See p. 52 and onward for instructions.

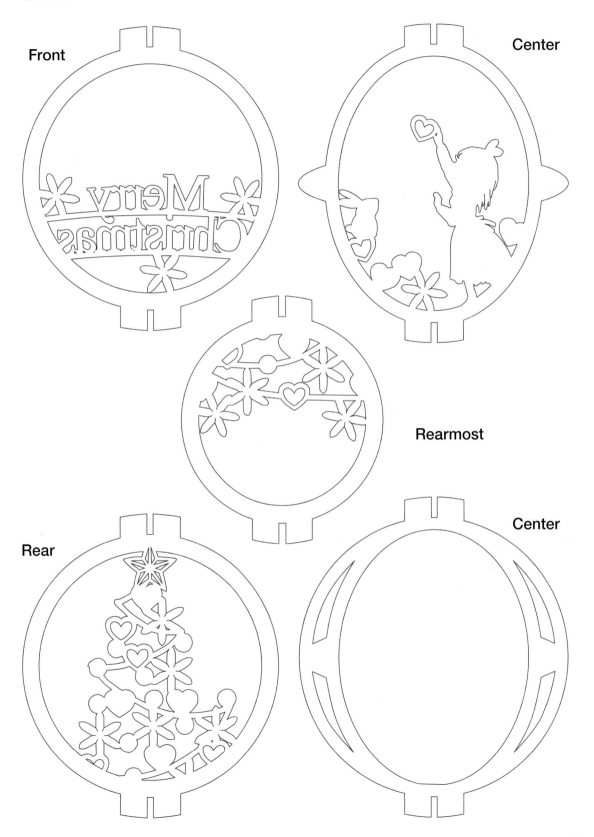

Front

Center

Rearmost

Rear

Center

Cut Here

Balloons and Girl Motif Rings

These motif rings are used for True Novice–through Advanced-level Spheres. See p. 52 and onward for instructions.

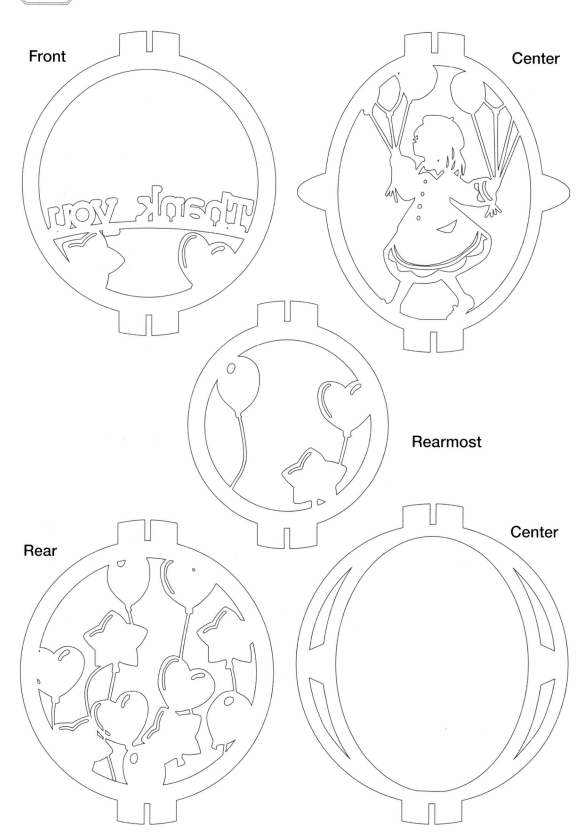

Front

Center

Rearmost

Rear

Center

Cut Here

92

P. 42

Gift Box Motif Rings

These motif rings are used for True Novice–through Advanced-level Spheres. See p. 52 and onward for instructions.

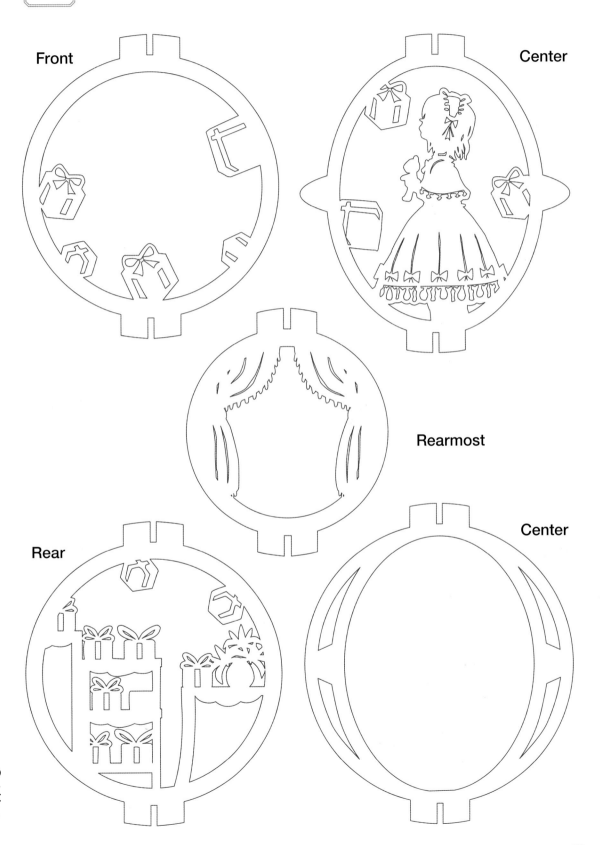

Front

Center

Rearmost

Rear

Center

Cut Here

P. 44

Zodiac Signs Motif Rings

These motif rings are used for True Novice–through Advanced-level Spheres. From pp. 95 through 100. See p. 52 and onward for instructions.

Center

Cut Here

Center

Cut Here

Zodiac Signs Motif Rings

Center

Center

Front

Rear

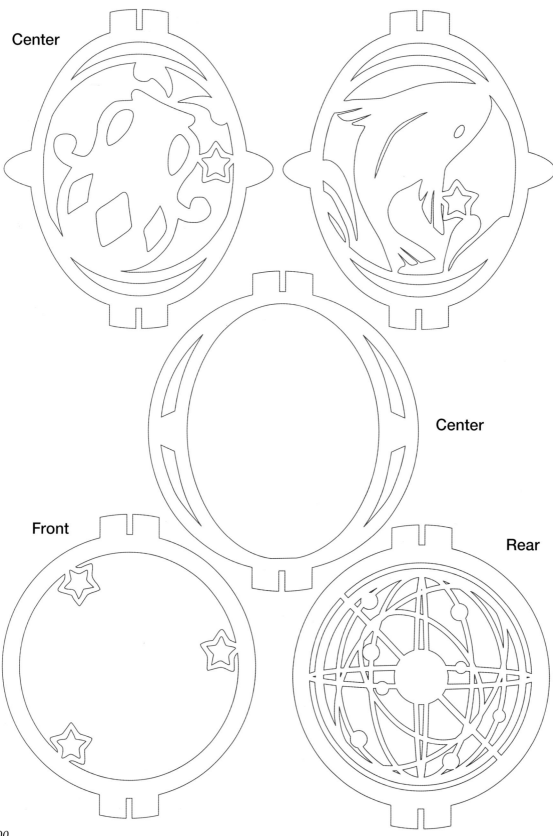

P. 52

True Novice–Level Ring Pieces
The ring pieces to construct True Novice level. See p. 52.

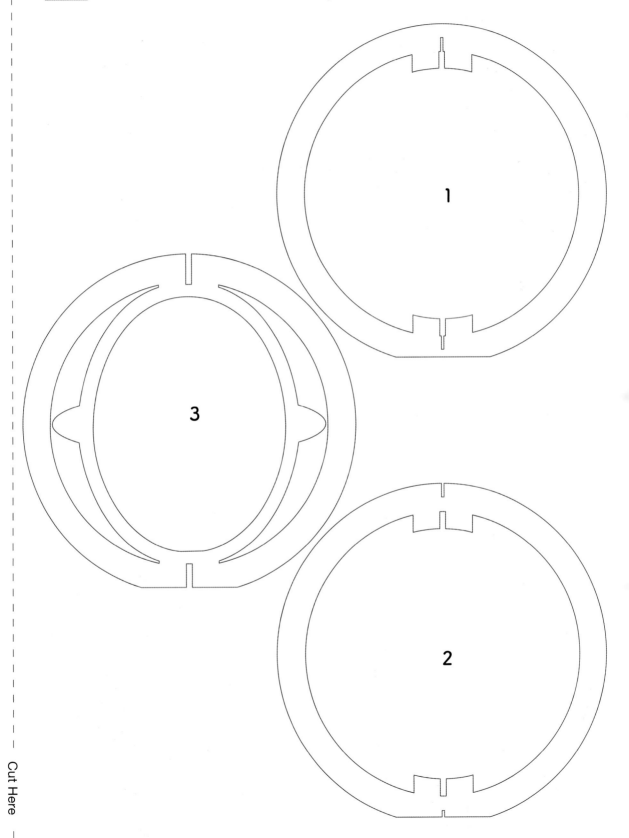

Cut Here

Beginner-Level Ring Pieces

Ring pieces to construct Beginner-level Spheres. From pp. 103 to 106. See p. 53 for instructions.

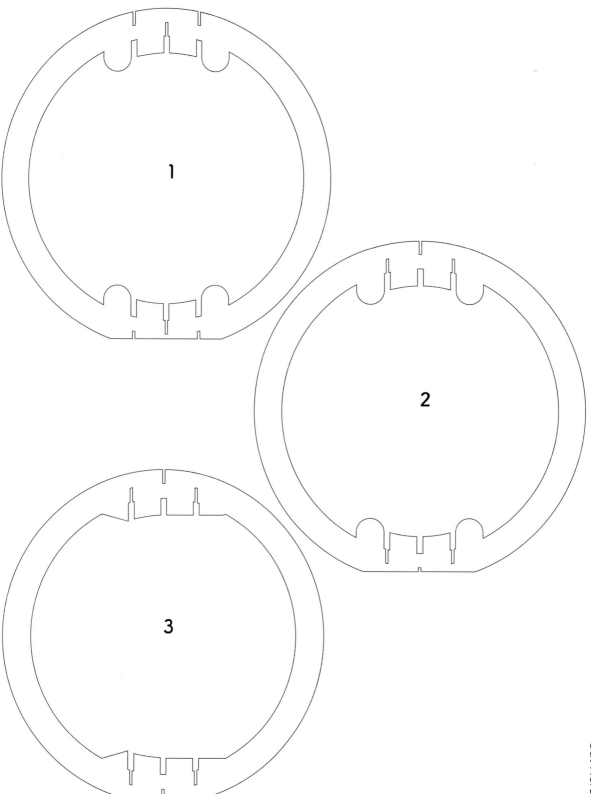

Cut Here

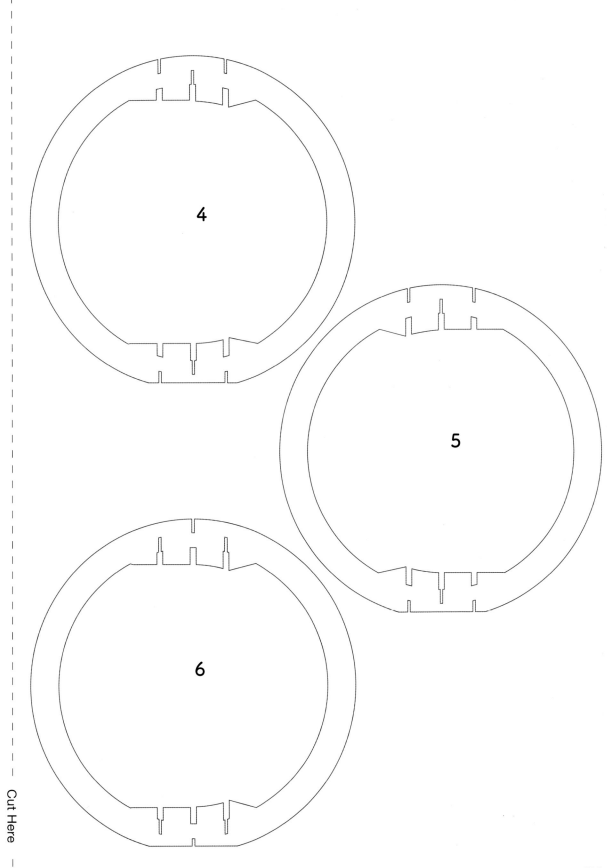

Cut Here

Intermediate-Level Ring Pieces

Ring pieces to construct Intermediate-level Spheres. From pp. 107 to 112. See p. 55 for instructions.

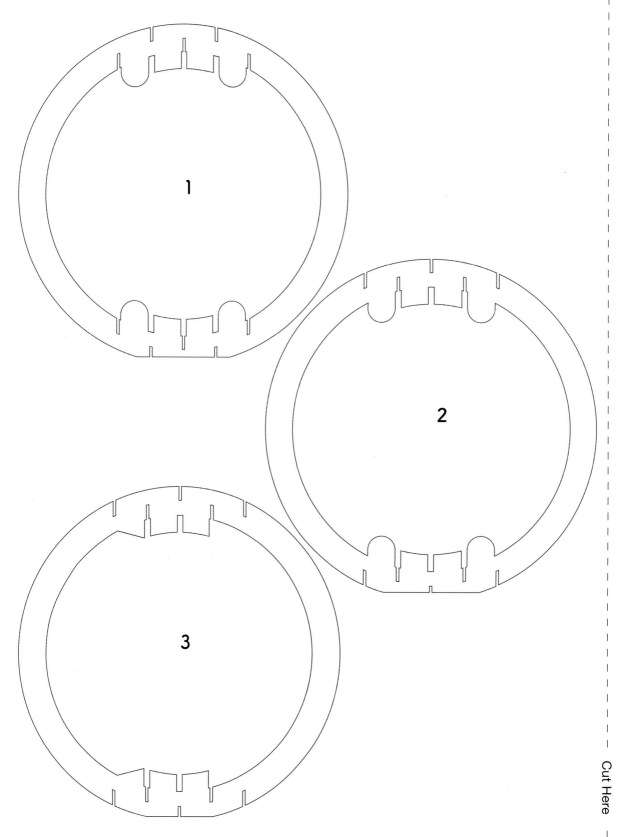

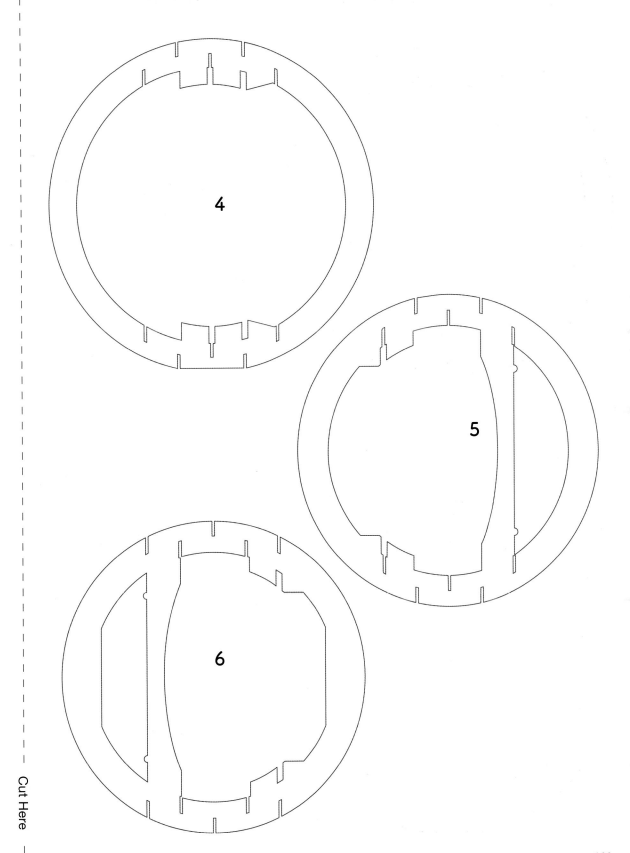

Cut Here

Cut Here

7

15

8

14

Advanced-Level Ring Pieces

Ring pieces to construct Advanced-level Spheres. From pp. 113 to 120. See p. 58 for instructions.

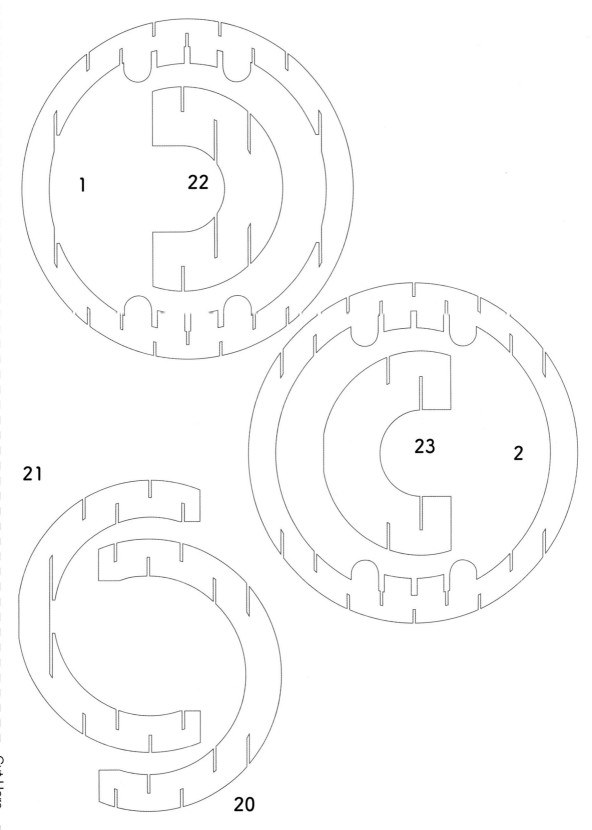

Cut Here

Advanced-Level Ring Pieces

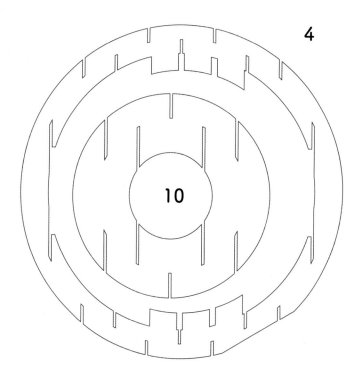

3

9

4

10

Cut Here

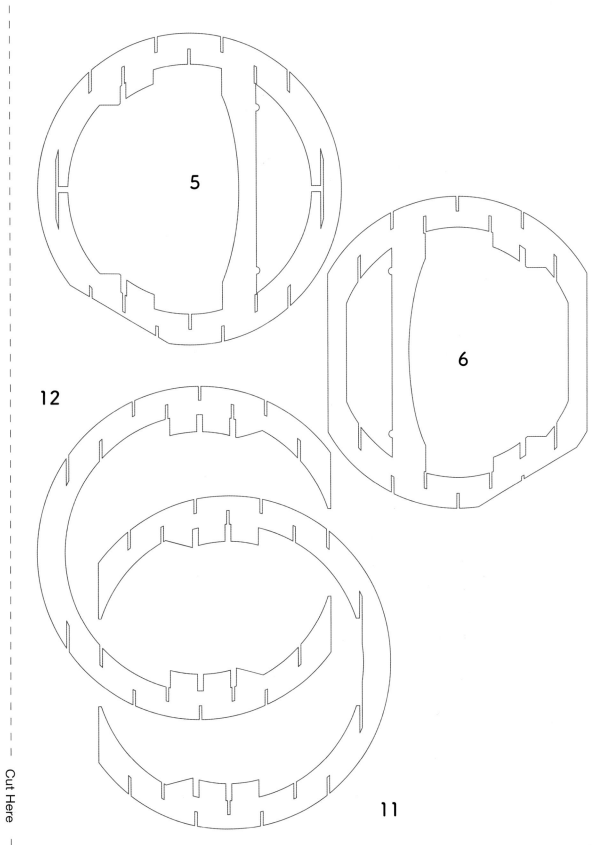

Cut Here

Advanced-Level Ring Pieces

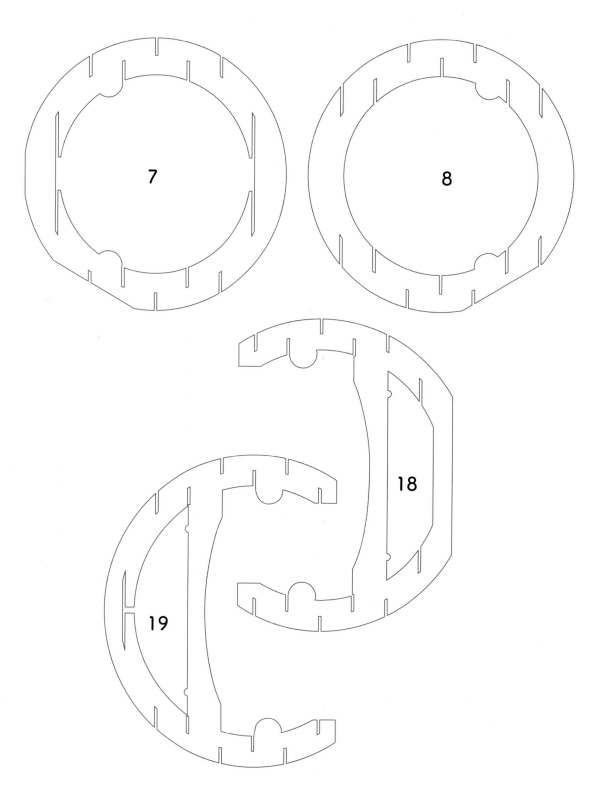

Expert-Level Ring Pieces with Door

Ring pieces to construct Expert-level Spheres with Doors. From pp. 121 to 128. See p. 62 for instructions.

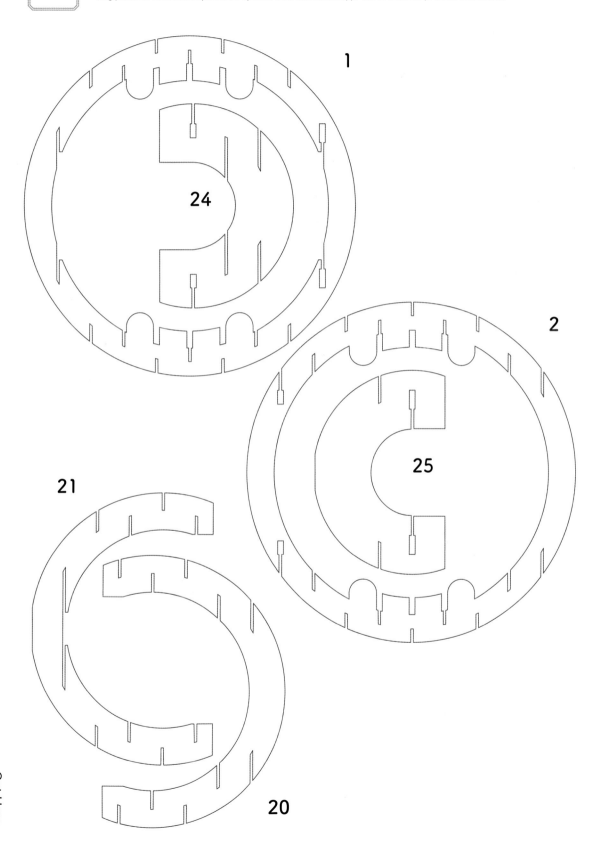

Cut Here

Expert-level Ring Pieces with Door

3

9

4

10

23

22

Cut Here

5

6

7

8

Cut Here

Expert Level-Ring Pieces with Door

12

11

19

18

Cut Here